Dr. Charles E. Fuller as He is Today

A VOICE FOR GOD
The Life of Charles E. Fuller
Originator of the Old Fashioned Revival Hour

By

WILBUR M. SMITH

WIPF & STOCK · Eugene, Oregon

Wipf and Stock Publishers
199 W 8th Ave, Suite 3
Eugene, OR 97401

A Voice for God
The Life of Charles E. Fuller
By Smith, Wilbur M.
ISBN 13: 978-1-62564-576-0
Publication date 1/8/2014
Previously published by W. A. Wilde, 1949

"My sole object is to do him justice."

J. G. Lockhart, in the Preface to his
Life of Sir Walter Scott

CONTENTS

	Preface	7
I.	On the Shores of Lake Champlain	13
II.	From New England to California	21
III.	From Boyhood Through College	42
IV.	In the Orange Groves	51
V.	Mrs. Grace Payton Fuller	58
VI.	The Great Change—Conversion	74
VII.	God's Quiet Leading at Placentia	86
VIII.	"Brought Very Low"	104
IX.	Girdling the Globe with the Gospel	110
X.	The Sweetest Voice in America	141
XI.	The Fuller Evangelistic Foundation	156
XII.	The Great Mass Meetings	168
XIII.	Fuller Theological Seminary	176
XIV.	A Recent Programme of the Old Fashioned Revival Hour	200
XV.	Charles E. Fuller the Man	214

PREFACE

It has been necessary to consult almost an entire library to obtain something of an adequate background for many of the subjects discussed in this book, and it would not be fair if I did not mention some of the works to which I am most deeply indebted. For the history of the Lake Champlain area, I have used almost exclusively the most recent and probably most authentic volume on this interesting part of our country, *Lake Champlain and Lake George,* by Frederic F. Van de Water, and I am grateful to its publishers, the Bobbs-Merrill Company, for permission to quote from its pages. Ingersoll's *Century Annals of San Bernardino County, 1769–1904,* has proved of great help to me in the early history of this part of Southern California. For early California, and especially Los Angeles county, I have depended for the most part on the following: Ray Allen Billington: *Westward Expansion,* Macmillan, 1949; an older work, Seymour Dunbar: *History of Travel in America,* published by the Bobbs-Merrill Co., Indianapolis, 1915 (particularly Vol. IV); the two standard works by Dr. Robert Glass Cleland: *From Wilderness to Empire,* published by Knopf in 1944, and his earlier *History of California, The American Period,* 1922. There are some fascinating pages in *The Boom of the 80's in Southern California,* by Glen S. Dumke, published by the Huntington Library of San Marino, California. On the city of Los Angeles, I have found most helpful: Theodore S. Van Dyke: *Southern California;* a work called simply *California* by Morrow Mayo, published in 1933; and the excellent volume in the American Guide Series, *Los Angeles,* published in 1941 by Hastings House of New York. On Pomona College, the standard work is *The Story of Pomona College,* by Charles Burt Sumner. For the history of Oregon, and the parents of Mrs. Fuller, the most helpful volume by far has been a work published in 1943 by Professor Robert Moulton Gatke: *Chronicles of Willamette, the Pioneer University of the West;* for general background, *Farthest Reach, Oregon and Washington,* published by Knopf in 1946; and, also very helpful, Dr. Olof Larsell's recent volume: *The Doctor in Oregon,* published by the Oregon Historical Society.

In writing the chapter on theological seminaries, I have used too many volumes to mention here, but wish to particularly give thanks to Dr. John Terrill Wayland, of North Wilkesboro, North Carolina, for allowing me to read his magnificent doctoral thesis, *The Theological Department in Yale College* (submitted in 1933).

For the history of the development of radio and the radio business, I have depended, for the most part, on the following: Dr. Gleason L. Archer: *History of Radio to 1926* (American Historical Society, New York, 1938); W. Rupert Maclaurin: *Invention and Innovation in the Radio Industry* (Macmillan, 1949); Robert J. Landry: *This Fascinating Radio Business* (Bobbs-Merrill, 1946); an earlier work: *The Electric Word: The Rise of Radio* (Macmillan, 1934); and a work still earlier, *Radio and Its Future,* edited by Martin Codel, and published by Harpers in 1930. I am grateful to Harper and Brothers for permission to use some brief quotations from a significant volume published by them in 1948, *The Communication of Ideas,* a series of addresses edited by Lyman Bryson, and published by the Institute for Religious and Social Studies. Helpful also has been the work by Francis Chase, Jr., *Sound and Fury,* published by Harper in 1942.

On the orange industry, there is nothing to compare in exhaustiveness with the first three chapters of the first volume of the great work, *The Citrus Industry,* by Herbert

PREFACE   9

John Weber, published by the University of California Press in 1948.

As usual whenever I write a book, I am greatly indebted to Dr. Kenneth S. Gapp, Librarian of Princeton Theological Seminary, for graciously allowing me to borrow a number of volumes, in this case relating particularly to early theologians and theological seminaries in this country.

For genealogical matters relating to the Day and Wright families, I am completely indebted to Miss Helen M. Spafford of Pomona, California. For the early history of the Fuller family, from the time they came over from Olney three centuries ago, I have received most help from a genealogical work published some years ago in New England, *Genealogy of Some of the Descendants of Thomas Fuller of Woburn*, by William Hyslop Fuller. Mrs. Elsie B. Chatterton, Librarian at the Bixby Memorial Free Library of Vergennes, Vermont, has very kindly sent me such information as can be gathered regarding Mr. Henry Fuller's residence in that city. Miss Katherine Anderson of the Library Association of Portland called my attention to a number of important items concerning early medical history on the Pacific Coast that I would otherwise have missed. I am indebted also for excellent references to Mr. Thomas Gillies, Assistant Librarian of Willamette University, Salem, Oregon. Mr. D. F. Cox of the Fuller Foundation very kindly drew up a complete list of the evangelists identified with the Fuller Foundation during the last five years, which I used in extensive correspondence. I have also to thank Miss Louise Deimel of Oakland, California, for obtaining for me a copy of F. W. Grant's *The Mysteries of the Kingdom of Heaven*. A great number of people in this country have sent me important letters, and such as have been used are given full credit in the following pages.

The late Mr. A. H. Albers was very generous in his assistance during the earlier days of writing this book, and since his death his secretary, Miss Irene Hagen, has been equally kind in supplying necessary information relating to technical matters in the broadcast of the Old Fashioned Revival Hour. I also wish to thank Mr. Frank McNamee of Fullerton, California, for many years an officer in the church which Dr. Fuller served at Placentia, who has given me a great deal of information regarding those early days. Dr. Bernard Ramm, of the faculty of the Bible Institute of Los Angeles, obtained for my use the only set of catalogs existing in any library in this country of the Bible Institute of Los Angeles during the years Dr. Fuller was a member of its Board of Trustees. Valuable material concerning Dr. Fuller's student days at Pomona College was obtained for me by Miss Luella Brooks, of the library staff at Pomona. I also wish to thank Miss Demond, Reference Librarian of the Smiley Public Library, Redlands, for her generous help. Mr. Leland Green has given me invaluable suggestions which are incorporated in the text of this biography. Both author and publishers are indebted to Dr. J. Elwin Wright, for permission to use two plates which were used in his very interesting work, the *Old Fashioned Revival Hour.*

Above all, I wish to express my deep appreciation to Mrs. Charles E. Fuller for her patience with me in answering scores upon scores of questions, and for placing in my hands important files of letters and information concerning the earlier days of her parents' pioneer struggles, and her own life immediately before and in the years that followed her marriage to Dr. Fuller. Without her help, I would not have attempted the writing of this volume.

Dr. Henry Clay Trumbull, founder and brilliant editor of the *Sunday School Times,* used to say that in heaven believers will be given the opportunity of doing work they did not find time for doing on earth. Some have even said that we will there write books that we did not have the opportunity of writing here. I do not know whether or not there will be any activity like that in the life to come—I am sure many hope there will not be—but if there is, there will be written among other works a grand dictionary of Christian biography, in which will be recorded the lives of many faithful disciples of Christ whose records are not found in our great biographical dictionaries constructed from a worldly viewpoint. It is strange that that great missionary, whose prayers and faithfulness molded the lives of thousands of candidates for the mission field, and brought thousands of Chinese to Christ as Saviour, Hudson Taylor, is not to be found in the thirty volumes of the *Dictionary of National Biography;* and neither C. I. Scofield nor R. A. Torrey, among many others, are to be found in the twenty-one volumes of our own *Dictionary of American Biography*. When this work is written, if it should be, we will then know of sufferings, struggles, victories, joys, prayers, conversions, visions, and miracles which are now unrecorded, and we will have them before us in a style of such beauty and with such a fullness and insight that escapes us all when we attempt to write in our feeble way. Any life which, when ending, receives the final encomium of the risen Lord, "Well done, thou good and faithful servant," would be a life worth writing, and from the reading of it blessing would naturally flow. It has been a privilege and blessing to have part in making this record of one of that great assembly of God's faithful servants, to men known or unknown, but to God alone perfectly known and remembered forever.

San Marino, California

Chapter I

ON THE SHORES OF LAKE CHAMPLAIN

"This is Charles E. Fuller speaking." For fifteen years these words have been heard every Lord's Day, for most of that time from one end of our continent to the other, often twice on the Lord's Day, in the Pilgrim Hour and the Old Fashioned Revival Hour, and again by great multitudes throughout the week, by transcription. For a quarter of a century if we may go back to his *first* radio messages, the rich, compassionate, pleading voice proceeding from this man has brought to millions of people the truths of the Word of God, in simple language, carrying comfort, hope, encouragement, cleansing, light, peace, and joy, and, by the work of the Holy Spirit through this voice have thousands been brought out from the power of darkness into the kingdom and the light of God's Son. When one hears this short sentence, "This is Charles E. Fuller speaking," it means that, even as the New Testament commands, this message from God to men is being borne, not by some angel in the clouds, nor by some mist-enshrouded being in a deep cavern of the earth, as with the so-called Greek oracles of ancient times, but by a man "of like passions with us."

When the sentence is uttered, "This is Charles E. Fuller speaking," it means that here is a man, speaking to men, concerning certain truths which have been revealed to him in the Word of God, which he believes with deep conviction, and which have been confirmed to him in his own personal experience. It was Bishop Phillips Brooks, I think, who, many years ago, in his famous lectures on preaching delivered at Yale University, said that preaching was "divine truth through a personality." Now while millions have heard Dr. Fuller speak, and thousands have seen him personally in the huge mass meetings throughout our country where he has spoken, and in the great audiences gathered together every Lord's Day afternoon at Long Beach, and many have even shaken his hand and looked into his beneficent face, few, very few, know much about the early experiences, the divine leadings, the frequent walking through the valley of trouble, the growth of his ministry, the scope of the Old Fashioned Revival Hour, the work of the Fuller Foundation, and the great results which continue to be manifested from this ministry.

The purpose of this volume is to set forth, as adequately as space permits, and human language allows, something of the life of this man to whom, for a quarter of a century, our own nation, and so many in other parts of the earth have listened with rich spiritual profit. I trust all my readers will even be interested in the early days of Dr. Fuller's father and mother, the growth of the state of California, in which he was born, and has lived and carried on his work, and even something of the orange grove industry in which he spent his earlier years of discipline, as well as everything (for which we have space) regarding his beloved wife, whom he often introduces as having "the sweetest voice in America," and her parents and their early struggles. From all of this has God molded, chastened, taught, and so mightily used, this servant of God, and the one chosen to be his ever-faithful helpmate.

There are three factors which exercise the most dominant influence over the life, and work, and character of every man and woman born into this world; namely, the physical, moral, and intellectual qualities of one's parents; the environment into which one is born; and, the education one is privileged to have, if any. For the child of God, there is a fourth factor, the supernatural power of the grace of God, manifested first in regeneration, and then continued in its sovereign, overruling, energizing, indwelling, and directing of life. In some mysterious way, not only do we derive from our parents, by the interaction of what biologists call genes, chromosomes, etc., our physical characteristics, our height, our health, the color of our hair and eyes, the length of our fingers, the contours of our face, but, in even a deeper mystery, not from genes, there enter into us certain fibres of character, good or bad, the germs of talents and capacities, prophecies of what one may be in the years to follow.

The ancestors of Charles E. Fuller were, none of them, as far as can be ascertained, nationally famous, but they were locally prominent. The line is not that of men of genius, but of ingenuity, and, which is better, men of honor. He was not born of a leisure-loving, wealthy line, but of successful, thrifty, hard-working landowners. His ancestors formed a continuous procession of pioneers, leaving England early in the seventeenth century for America, leaving New England in the next century for the western shores of Lake Champlain, and leaving New York in the next century for California. Pioneers are men of courage, men whose faith and hope is in the future, men of great endurance and strength, and, if successful, as many pioneers were not, necessarily men of ingenuity, with a capacity for leadership.

Olney, in Buckinghamshire, England, fifty-five miles northwest of London, on the Owse River, has been identified for nearly two centuries in the minds of Christians with the famous Olney hymns, written by John Newton, the curate in that tiny village from 1764 to 1779, assisted by the equally famous poet, William Cowper, also a resident of the same village from 1767–1786.

The Fuller line from which Charles E. Fuller came was

founded in this country by John Fuller, who, after a residence in Olney of undetermined length, sailed from England in the great exodus of Puritans early in the seventeenth century, and soon settled with his family in Lynn, Massachusetts, ten miles northeast of Boston. His son Edward (1621–1695) was probably the most distinguished of this line of Fullers, being a representative from Lynn in 1655 and again in 1674–1678, and a Lieutenant in King Philip's War. James, the great-grandfather of Charles E. Fuller, who lived to the age of ninety-four, after moving to various cities in New Hampshire and Vermont, finally came in 1819 to Peru, New York, on the shores of Lake Champlain, bringing with him his large family, including his son James, who was then eighteen years of age.

We must now tarry for a moment on the western shores of this lovely body of water, famous, one regrets to say, for at least two centuries, more for war than for its beauty or its commercial traffic. As the latest authority on the northernmost of the great five lakes has said, "For the first two hundred years of Lake George's and Lake Champlain's recorded existence, and still further back through the dimness of Indian tales, the principal traffic of the lakes was martial. The chief enterprise of the area they drained was battle. Their nature and situation bent history and channeled the course of empire." Lake Champlain was discovered by the famous French explorer of that name in 1609. For nearly three-quarters of a century, 1690–1761, the French and Indians fought back and forth on these shores—Mohawk, Iroquois, Huron, Algonquin tribes, savage, brutal, merciless. France claimed this territory because she discovered it. England claimed it because the Iroquois were her allies. When King George's War ended in 1748, the Canadians had already built several forts along the lake, including Fort William Henry, and Fort Ticonderoga, both of which were to see many bloody battles; in fact, as the author we have just quoted well

ON THE SHORES OF LAKE CHAMPLAIN   17

remarks, "The things that had driven thousands in flight from Europe was moving westward to overtake them. The recurrent wars of the old world were spreading to encompass the new. Conflicts that established by their treaties fresh grievances, which begot new campaigns, had become the nation's prime industry, and the need of the standing armies that had supplanted the old feudal levies, drew upon entire populations. The wilderness in which the harried had sought peace was about to become the site of wars more savage than Europe's." The shore and islands of this lake had been stained for over a century now with the blood of Indians and white men and women, scalped, tortured, shot, cut to pieces, and when the armies were stationed in these early forts, they would again and again suffer from scurvy, dysentery, typhus, smallpox, and the terrible winter cold. Here again, just before our Fuller family came to live on its western shores, there was fought in the War of 1812, the Battle of Lake Champlain in September, 1814, which, said Admiral Mahan, "more nearly than any other incident of the War of 1812, merits the epithet, 'decisive.' " Lake Champlain forms, for one hundred miles, the New York-Vermont boundary line—322 of its 490 square miles are in Vermont, 151 in New York, and 17 in Canada.

In 1819, James Fuller, as we have said, moved from the well-settled state on the eastern shore, Vermont, to the sparsely-populated New York side, near what is now called Peru, five miles south of the city that has since grown up, Plattsburg. To James Fuller, on January 12, 1846, twins were born, Henrietta and Henry, the latter being the father of the subject of our biography, one who was to live a strenuous, remarkable life for eighty years, that was to span the North American continent. Indeed, the seven successive male ancestors of Charles E. Fuller lived each an average of seventy-eight years. The principal occupation of the western shores of

Lake Champlain in the first half of the nineteenth century, in addition to general agriculture, in which wheat was the prime crop, was the raising of sheep, especially up to the end of first half of the century, when, with the increasing competition of the west, the valley farmers turned more and more to the raising of cattle.

Along the rich and beautiful western slopes of Lake Champlain lived Rufus Day (1783–1838) and his extensive family, including six sons, of whom five built homes for themselves, when coming to manhood, touching the shore at Bluff Point, each house identical in structure to their father's residence, which they seemed to have thought was just about perfect. Among these five sons was Edmund (1816–1864), who, by his wife Maria Wright Sturdevant, had a son Charles and two daughters, Elma and Helen. It is unnecessary here to dwell at any length on the history of the Day family,[1] but three items, it seems to me, are too important to leave in the buried tomes of New England genealogy. The great-grandfather of Rufus Day was Robert Day (1684–1742) who, when he passed away in Killingly, Connecticut, had the following lines inscribed on his tombstone:

> "I sought the Lord in early youth,
> Nor did I seek in vain.
> He led me in the paths of truth,
> And great has been my gain."

The grandfather of this Robert Day was another Robert Day (1605–1683), apparently the most famous of all, "having sailed to Ipswich, Massachusetts, in 1635 on the good ship Hope Well, Captain Burdick." He took the freeman's oath, and in 1650 became a select man on the jury of Ipswich, and

---

[1] The Assessment Roll in Peru, as far back as 1798, in a list of approximately twenty names, assigns more than a third to the Day clan, listing the following sons of Amos Day: Ezra, the father of Henry Day; Asa, the father of R. P. and Doris Day; Theron, father of William Day; Amos Day, Jr. and Rufus Day, father of Cyrus, Edmund, Nelson and David Day.

in 1660 was appointed a constable. A citizen of New England could only claim the right to the title freeman, when, among other things, he was a reputable member of some Congregational church. Persons were made freemen by the general court of the colony, and also by quarterly courts of the county. None but freemen could hold office or vote for rulers.

We mentioned above that Edmund Day, grandfather of Charles Fuller on his mother's side, married Maria Wright Sturdevant, whose mother was Jurusha Wright, the wife of Elias Sturdevant. This Wright line was a military one indeed. Daniel Wright was a notable soldier for three years in the Revolutionary War, and fought again in the War of 1812, when he held the high position of Lieutenant Colonel, and finally advanced to the rank of Brigadier General. "It has been said that in the line of sturdy Sturdevants, the same quiet energy, persistent perseverance, honest industry, self-reliance, regard for truth, belief in the ultimate triumph of right, and tendency to independent thinking, have prevailed in every generation."

Of such worthy ancestors, coming over from noble England, near the beginning of the seventeenth century, to brave the hardships of New England, and to lay so solidly the foundations of our own great nation—hard-working, locally-honored men, brave in war, living without scandal or shame, and their faithful, lovely wives, enduring equal hardship, wholly devoid of the comforts which all of us now enjoy, making their own clothes, preparing their own meat, milling their own flour, erecting cabins, houses, and barns, protecting their loved ones as they worked with guns slung across their shoulders, God-fearing, honest men of the soil, of such did God raise up this great radio evangelist in another era, which, though filled with the marvels of invention, was likewise marked by war, two awful wars, more dreadful than his ancestors ever dreamed of, and embracing greater areas than were even then to be found upon the maps of navigators.

In the town of Peru, the Fuller family helped build the old Methodist church in 1832, where services are still held. Of the two families, at this time, however, the Fullers were only nominal in their church relationship, while the Days were devout members. Probably because there was not enough opportunity for building up an independent business in what was then a rather sparsely settled community, Henry Fuller, with his wife Helen Maria Day, whom he had married September 10, 1867, moved to Vergennes, Vermont, where the young husband began working in the town's general store. Vergennes, by the way, twenty miles south of the larger and more famous city of Burlington, has the distinction of being the oldest and smallest city in Vermont. With great care and thrifty habits, which were to attend him throughout his life, and to be passed on to his son, Charles, the young married couple were soon able to build a home. In the years that followed, he built and superintended an excelsior factory. However, though he came from a long sturdy line, Henry Fuller's health was not of the best, and news coming to him, as it came to all New England, that the nearest climate to paradise on the North American continent was to be found in California, at the age of twenty-nine, with the pioneer spirit of his forefathers running in his blood, he undertook a trip to that far off land, that was to prove infinitely more significant in the remaining years of his life than he at that time could possibly imagine. Whether someone near him had been to California, or he had read accounts of the so-called Eden of the United States in some newspaper, or some advertising folder had fallen into his hands, we do not know, but California for the Fuller family is another chapter, and to that fascinating subject we must now turn.

CHAPTER II

FROM NEW ENGLAND TO CALIFORNIA

California! No word, geographical or otherwise, can be found in the 450 years of the history and literature of North America so connative of the hopes and dreams of men as this smooth-flowing, five-syllable word, the (probable) meaning of its origin, however, being one which Californians have never chosen to publicize, namely, *hot furnace*. For a century, around the world, California has conveyed to every mind two images—gold and oranges. Nothing could be more suggestive for promotional purposes than the name Golden State—the desert with its mysteries, the mountains with their beauty and difficulties of ascent, a thousand miles of coast line lapped by the waters of the Pacific, on the other side of which is the Orient, gorgeous flowers, golden fruit, a salubrious climate, and the assurance, so many have said, of long life—this is California. Who could want more? Then with the dawn of the twentieth century, in addition to a vast influx, literally, of millions of people, esoteric and theosophical cults began to flourish, followed by the age of the movies, with Hollywood—an incarnation of only one aspect of California life, thank God—and then oil, spurting up from the ground, hundreds of millions of dollars worth of it, often called "black gold." We cannot in any accurate way begin to comprehend the meaning of the early years of Charles E. Fuller, without briefly recalling the strange, almost miraculous, ever-changing, certainly marvelous history of this most fascinating of all the states of the union.

Less than thirty years after Columbus' first voyage to North

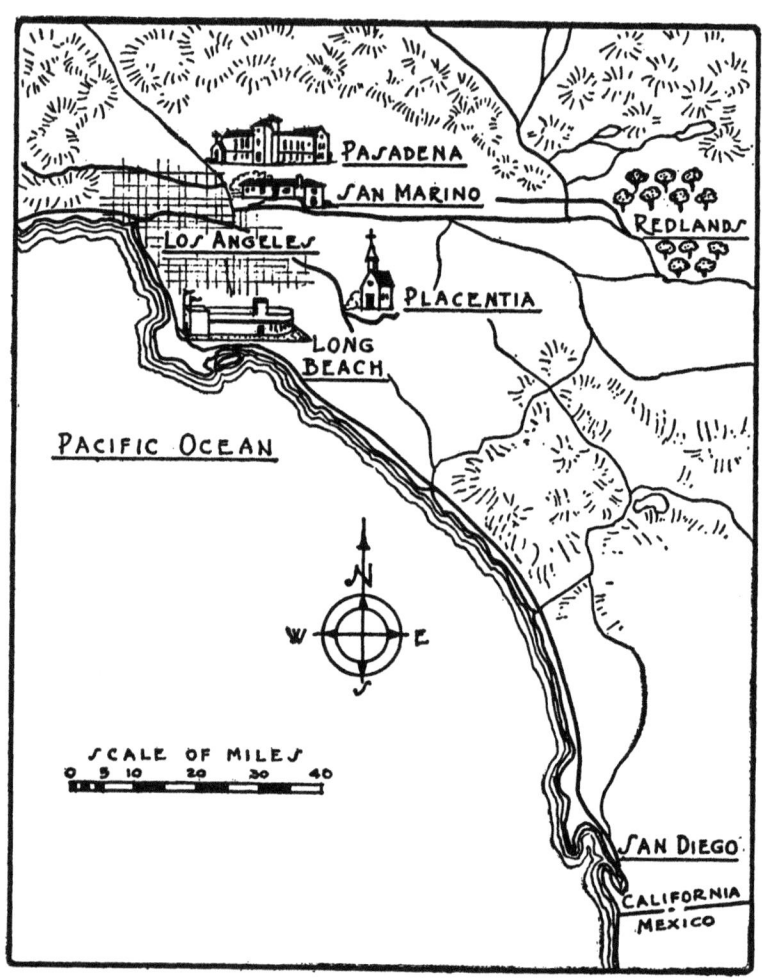

America, Cortes conquered Mexico, in 1519. By 1532–1533, the Spaniards had discovered what is now called Lower California, a barren peninsula that for many years was to remain an irresistible magnet of mystery to these adventurers, who thought its mountains held gold and precious stones, and that its waters were continually washing up pearls upon the shore, some even believing that here was the kingdom of the Amazons. One writer went so far as to say that it "lay at the right hand of the Indies . . . very close to the Terrestrial Paradise." This ever-alluring word, Paradise, and its twin, Eden, continually appear and reappear in both the early and later literature of California. In 1535 Cortes named the land *California*. A Portuguese navigator in Spanish service, Juan Rodriquez Cabrillo, discovered San Pedro Bay, but sixty years would pass before another ship would explore this area. *Two full centuries* passed before the first of the twenty-one famous Spanish missions was founded, when in 1769 Father Serra founded the Mission San Diego de Alcala.

At the northern end of the state, which, by the way, is 780 miles long, varying from 150 to 350 miles in width, the mission and presidio of San Francisco was established. As with this city, *San* being the word for *Saint,* and *Francisco* a variation of the word *Francis,* so numerous other names in this land of flowers, are the marks of the early Catholic missions; even its most famous city, Los Angeles, carrying a name, *not too accurate,* meaning the *City of Angels.* It was just about this time—to be exact, on the early morning of September 4, 1781, that an expedition, organized by the new governor of California, Felipe de Neva, set out from the San Gabriel Mission for the official founding of Los Angeles, the governor leading a procession consisting of soldiers, forty-four settlers, some priests, and a few Indian acolytes. When they came to the spot which the Indians had named Yang-na, they stopped, the governor made a speech, and the city of now two million people was born in the midst of barbaric simplicity. We will come back to this city's later history in another chapter of this book.

It was not until 1791, 255 years after the discovery of Lower California, 170 years after the Mayflower had arrived on the rocky New England coast, two years after the inauguration of George Washington as the first President of the United States, that the first American reached the Golden State—John Groehm (Graham), who, on the very day he stepped ashore at Monterey Bay, September 13, suddenly died from exhaustion and exposure. Five years later, the Yankee skipper, Ebenezer Door, brought his ship, the *Otter,* into Monterey Bay, the first American ship ever to enter Californian waters. For some decades a vast trade had been carried on in sealskins; in fact, so important had the trade become that Russia grew increasingly insistent that the waters of northern California belonged to her, and her seal traders, a political question into which we cannot enter here. The great ranches throughout California were engaged principally in raising cattle, but California could not make use of all the vast herds roaming its rich lands, and they welcomed these New England traders, who bought hides and tallow for the growing boot and shoe industry of the colonial states, especially for Lynn. Occasionally in the early 30's there would be as many as twenty-five or thirty ships at one time in San Francisco harbor, waiting for their load of merchandise. The trip from Boston to California—(and sometimes to China) around the Cape and back to Boston—took from two to three years, with storms, the possibility of mutiny, the customary dysentery and scurvy, monotonous ship's diet, and high duties, for some of these cargoes paid a duty as high as twenty-five thousand dollars.

When the power of Spain was finally broken over the southern part of what is now North America, and Mexico became

FROM NEW ENGLAND TO CALIFORNIA 25

independent, on September 26, 1822, California was proclaimed a province of the southern empire, and remained such until the close of the Mexican War. Slowly, Americans from the Atlantic coastal states were irresistibly drawn to the other side of the continent, to take up their residence, and find their fortune (or lose all they had) in this land that was soon to become, literally, the state of gold. The first trail-blazer to complete the overland journey from the east to the west was Jedediah Strong Smith, a fearless pioneer, who, at the same time, was a devout Christian. Smith was employed by the Rocky Mountain Fur Company. He left the great Salt Lake on August 22, 1826, and arrived at San Gabriel, a few miles east of what is now Los Angeles, on November 27. Continuing his journey north into Oregon, he met Dr. McLaughlin in the Willamette Basin the following year, a name that will reappear in another chapter of this book. Jedediah Smith was a man of prayer, with a fine education, and a great knowledge of the Word of God, which he often quoted in his letters and journal. His latest biographer says, "He was like Stonewall Jackson, in combining with the most ardent belief in and practice of the Christian religion, an undaunted courage, fierce and impetuous nature, and untiring energy."

The Yankees, coming into California, as one would expect, by sharp trading, by attending to business, by native genius for increasing their wealth, were in many places becoming masters of enterprises which the Mexicans and Spaniards thought belonged to them. Tension developed in the north, and in the south. Shots were fired, blood was spilled. In 1840 an order was issued that *no American would be allowed to take up residence in California,* unless he was married to a California woman. In 1845, all immigration to California was legally forbidden. How weak such legal barriers become when the mighty rivers of "manifest destiny" come sweeping over the cataracts of the years. On May 13, 1846—whether just or unjust it is not our business here to debate—the Mexican War began. Mexico was too weak to hold out for any length of time against her strong and united northern neighbor: in a year and a half the war was over, and on February 2, 1848, California was ceded to the United States.

Few people may remember the year in which the Mexican War closed, but millions of citizens know of something else that took place in that same year, which was to change the face of all the west—the "discovery" of gold. Of course, the Indians long before this knew there was gold in California, and the Spaniards had found small deposits of this precious metal; in fact, as early as 1811 a sheepherder found gold in the Santa Feliciana Canyon, and sent twenty ounces of it to the Philadelphia mint. But even this, for some strange reason, did not create any excitement. Of the actual discovery of gold by one Marshall, January 24, 1848, we will have something to say in a subsequent chapter. There were no telegrams in those days, and news traveled slowly, but by 1849 the Atlantic Coast knew that gold had been found, and thousands of men that year, and in the few years that followed, led on by a power they could not resist, many selling all they had and even going into debt, many others leaving loved ones whom they would never see again, obtained transportation to that far-off state, either by ship, going around the Cape, enduring months of hardship, or crossing the continent, the deserts and the mountains, over land much of which had never before known the tread of a white man's foot. Thousands never got to California. Many more, when arriving, were almost too weak to endure the long days of toil necessary for extracting gold in these heretofore unknown streams. But on they came, wave after wave of them, and many stayed. Some grew rich, some made a living, some nearly starved to death, but gold is gold, and 1849 marked the beginning of the greatest migration across any country that the modern world has seen. This mass movement is still continuing; in fact, more people now come to California in one year than lived in all the United States at the time of the signing of the Declaration of Independence.

The more notable the visitors to California in the middle of the nineteenth century, the greater were the eulogies raised in behalf of the Golden State. The eminent New England theologian, Dr. Horace Bushnell, visited California in 1856, active in the search for a permanent home for the proposed College of California, and being offered, by unanimous vote of the Board of Trustees, the presidency of this yet unrealized institution, wrote back from San Jose: "The air is fresh and bracing, the clouds are flying in squadrons, and the shadows chasing across the landscape to give it life. As to the hills, nothing I have seen could match them or help me by comparison to describe them. Their covering is the intensest meadow-green, save that often the flowers are so profuse in spots that the green is covered. There the light streaming down their sides set off by the shadows of the clouds makes them fairly live. The flowers smiling in their silent beauty before God, and breathing out their incense to Him. Oh, it was the nearest thing to a Garden of Eden actually extant that I ever saw."

Others who came to the far southwest changed the figure of speech: instead of calling California a Garden of Eden, they referred to it as the new Palestine. In 1867 there came to California a man who, just past the age of forty, was in subsequent years to write two books that would go through many editions. I refer to the philanthropist and scholar, Charles Loring Brace, a friend of Lord Bryce, Emerson, Theodore Parker, Henry Ward Beecher, the botanist Asa Gray, John Stuart Mill, and even Charles Darwin. Many a minister has on his shelves one or both of his two most famous books, *Gesta Christi, A History of Humane Progress Under Christianity*, and *The Unknown God*.

As a result of his California sojourn, Brace wrote a volume, now almost forgotten, *The New West*, which Putnam published in 1869. Toward the end, he has a chapter called, "The American Palestine," in which he enlarges upon Deuteronomy 8:7–10: "For Jehovah thy God bringeth thee into a good land, a land of brooks of water, of fountains and springs, flowing forth in valleys and hills; a land of wheat and barley, and vines and fig-trees, and pomegranates: a land of olive trees and honey: a land wherein thou shalt eat bread without scarceness, thou shalt not lack anything in it; a land whose stones are iron, and out of whose hills thou mayest dig copper. And thou shalt eat and be full, and thou shalt bless Jehovah, thy God for the good land which he hath given thee." Brace said that California, like Palestine, had suffered such devastations as are depicted in the prophecy of Joel, that it has salt lakes, hot springs, deposits of bitumen, and earthquakes. "I have often wondered," he continued, "whether the Asiatic climate of California would hereafter produce any mind on whom nature would stamp itself as it did on the wonderful Hebrew poets, or who could be thus inspired by devotion and worship." He has an anecdote we ought not to forget regarding Los Angeles, i.e., the City of Angels: "I asked a Catholic priest with whom I was traveling if it (Los Angeles) deserved its name. He replied that the Holy Scriptures inform us there are two kinds of angels, the good and the bad, and of the latter he thought there was no want in the place."

The gold rush precipitated the problem of better transportation and mail service. In that year of 1848, contracts were let for semi-monthly mail service between New York and San Francisco, but thirty days elapsed between the time a letter started out on its journey, and its arrival at the

FROM NEW ENGLAND TO CALIFORNIA

western city. Today one can mail a letter in Boston on Monday morning, and delivery in San Francisco or Los Angeles may be counted upon the following morning. Ten years later, in September, 1858, the first transcontinental stage coach route was established, with a fare of two hundred dollars; mail cost from two to ten dollars an ounce. These were the days when the whole fabulous legend of stage coaches and their drivers, and wild outlaws, originated. By 1870, the stage coaches were doomed, for "the iron horse" had come in, and railroads were spanning our land. The Union Pacific began laying tracks toward the east, as the Central Pacific began laying tracks toward the west, by mutual agreement, in 1863. In four years, 1864–1867, only 116 miles were laid! A fast Sante Fe train now *in fifteen minutes* travels over the length of track which it took the whole year of 1864 to lay. On May 10, 1869, the final spike of the first transcontinental railroad was driven at Promontory, Utah. In 1883, the Atchison, Topeka, and Santa Fe, and Northern Pacific had also laid tracks across the country. Five days and nights were travelers cooped up in these trains from the Missouri River to Southern California, traveling at the rate of twenty-two miles an hour.

Inasmuch as the father of the subject of this biography will soon be on one of these trains himself, that we might have some idea of the conditions endured by men and women then traveling, let us reread Robert Louis Stevenson's reminiscences in his now seldom seen work *The Amateur Emigrant:* "At Ogden (Utah) we changed cars from the Union Pacific to the Central Pacific line of railroad. The change was doubly welcome, for, first, we had better cars on the new line; and, second, those in which we had been cooped for more than ninety hours had begun to stink abominably. Several yards away, as we returned, let us say from dinner, our nostrils were assailed by rancid air. I have stood on a platform while the whole train was shunting; and, as the dwelling-cars drew near, there would come a whiff of pure menagerie, only a little sourer, as from men instead of monkeys. I think we are only human in virtue of open windows. Without fresh air, you only require a bad heart, and a remarkable command of the Queen's English, to become such another as Dean Swift; a kind of leering human goat, leaping and wagging your scut on mountains of offence. I do my best to keep my head the other way, and look for the human rather than the bestial in this Yahoo-like business of the emigrant train. But one thing I must say, the car of the Chinese was notably the least offensive."

It is time for us now to forget Monterey, San Francisco, the gold rush, and the stage coaches, and move down into Southern California, and watch the city of Los Angeles take shape, and learn something of the town into which Henry Fuller came in the year 1874.

Los Angeles, now the fifth largest city in the United States in population, and in area (451 square miles) the largest single municipality in the entire United States, was originally an Indian village called Yang-na. In 1769, just seven years before the Declaration of Independence, a party of explorers and missionaries from Mexico, under the leadership of Captain Gaspar de Portolá, discovered this Indian village, and decided that here a town should sooner or later be established. The great San Gabriel Mission was nine miles northeast of this spot. For the first eighty years one could say that nothing of any importance needing our attention took place in this immediate area, although by 1830, with twelve hundred people residing in its primitive buildings, most of adobe brick, it was the largest community in California. As late as 1846, less than three thousand people lived in this town. The entire sheep industry, which then gave this city much of its prosperity and activity, was wholly wiped out in the terrible drought of 1862–1864, but it immediately recovered, and by

FROM NEW ENGLAND TO CALIFORNIA 31

1868, property value in Los Angeles county was estimated at four million dollars. It was a rough city, like almost all western frontier towns before the days of the Civil War—which, by the way, hardly affected California. The rumor was that Los Angeles had a murder a day. Even at the present time, with its highly developed civilization, its vast system of educational institutions, and great wealth, Los Angeles probably displays more scandal and crime in its daily newspapers than any other city in the United States. Saloons two generations ago were so numerous that it is estimated there was one for every fifty inhabitants. Beginning in 1870, the population of Southern California increased at a phenomenal rate, probably more rapidly than that of any large area in the entire history of the United States, and Los Angeles was profoundly affected by this vast immigration. From 1870 to 1880, the population of Southern California increased 101 per cent; from 1880–1890, 212 per cent; in the next decade, 51 per cent; in the first ten years of our century, 147 per cent; in the second decade, 79 per cent; from 1920–1930, 117 per cent. During the forty years elapsing since 1900, the total population of Southern California increased 1101 per cent, but the population of Los Angeles increased 1535 per cent. As a well-informed writer on Southern California has said, "If the population of the United States had increased at a similar rate, we would today have a national population of 571,564,774."

Henry Fuller came to Los Angeles in 1874, when the population of the city was about 15,000, and the value of property in the county was estimated at $12,332,000. The city of Los Angeles alone enclosed about two thousand adobe houses, with a few erected here and there from wood—none of stone. There came into this so-called paradise of the western world just about this time, one of the most famous world travelers of that generation, of royal blood, Ludwig Louis

Salvator, Archduke of Austria, the son of Leopold II. Though only twenty-nine years of age, the Archduke had already seen all of Europe, some of Asia, and a large part of America. He wrote a book at this time called *Los Angeles in the 70's*, and what he said about the city is so important and so vividly written that we could not possibly have a better conception of the Los Angeles into which Henry Fuller came than by having some of his lines before us. "The climate is surpassed by no other region in the new world. Extremes of heat and cold are unknown; it is a land of perpetual spring. In winter the days are invariably comfortably warm; the nights in summer are delightfully cool—blankets, as a matter of fact, being essential at night throughout the summer season. It is possible to work outdoors in shirtsleeves from January to December, and there is no month of the year when fruit does not ripen or flowers bloom." The fact was that even this city, in its primitive state looked like a flower garden, for its streets and sidewalks were lined with pepper trees, eucalyptus and castor-bean trees, and here and there, weeping willows. "A gay crowd of men and animals is constantly going and coming in the streets. Innumerable bronze-colored half breeds from the Mexican province of Sonora, wearing plug hats on their dusky heads, tanned Scotchmen in straw helmets, distinguished Spaniards in riding clothes, and animated laughing girls in large cotton capes and broad straw hats passed by. The streets are at the peak of their activity in the evenings, especially at the entrance to the opera house, where there is so much business and shouting going on that it is difficult to get through."

With the completion of the transcontinental railroads, opening up the entire Far West to the millions of Americans living in the older New England and Atlantic states, a new fever of pioneering began to spread, infecting vast multitudes of both young and older men. The germ lodged in the mind

Salvator, Archduke of Austria, the son of Leopold II. Though only twenty-nine years of age, the Archduke had already seen all of Europe, some of Asia, and a large part of America. He wrote a book at this time called *Los Angeles in the 70's*, and what he said about the city is so important and so vividly written that we could not possibly have a better conception of the Los Angeles into which Henry Fuller came than by having some of his lines before us. "The climate is surpassed by no other region in the new world. Extremes of heat and cold are unknown; it is a land of perpetual spring. In winter the days are invariably comfortably warm; the nights in summer are delightfully cool—blankets, as a matter of fact, being essential at night throughout the summer season. It is possible to work outdoors in shirtsleeves from January to December, and there is no month of the year when fruit does not ripen or flowers bloom." The fact was that even this city, in its primitive state looked like a flower garden, for its streets and sidewalks were lined with pepper trees, eucalyptus and castor-bean trees, and here and there, weeping willows. "A gay crowd of men and animals is constantly going and coming in the streets. Innumerable bronze-colored half breeds from the Mexican province of Sonora, wearing plug hats on their dusky heads, tanned Scotchmen in straw helmets, distinguished Spaniards in riding clothes, and animated laughing girls in large cotton capes and broad straw hats passed by. The streets are at the peak of their activity in the evenings, especially at the entrance to the opera house, where there is so much business and shouting going on that it is difficult to get through."

With the completion of the transcontinental railroads, opening up the entire Far West to the millions of Americans living in the older New England and Atlantic states, a new fever of pioneering began to spread, infecting vast multitudes of both young and older men. The germ lodged in the mind

FROM NEW ENGLAND TO CALIFORNIA

of Henry Fuller, among others, and at the age of thirty-two, he decided he must see this romantic area. Ever noted for his thrift, he entered into an agreement to take a load of sheep from New England to California. He probably rode in the day coach, and watched over the sheep in the freight cars, but of this journey we have no record. One thing is clear: he was so impressed with California, that he decided to stay. In the following year he sent for his family, and together they set up housekeeping at Lordsburg, where they planned to raise wheat and turkeys. However, a severe drought scourged the land soon after they had invested everything they had in the venture, and they were reduced to extreme circumstances. To help keep the family going, Mrs. Fuller took farm-hands to board. The time came when all they had to eat were the rabbits which the head of the home shot in the fields of his burned-up farm.

Henry Fuller then turned to business, and moved to Los Angeles, where he set up the first first-class furniture store in that city, the initial stock consisting of two dozen rockers and ten dozen chairs. He had an inventive mind, and it is said he manufactured the first bed-spring in Los Angeles. This immediately brought a great increase in his business. A relative soon came out from the eastern states to join him, and together they manufactured furniture in a building that stood, until recently, near the Southern Pacific depot. While residing in Los Angeles, the great boom of 1885–1887 occurred, in which fortunes were made and lost. The real estate transactions of 1887 alone in Los Angeles county amounted to over two hundred million dollars! Of more than one hundred cities and towns laid out on paper to be established in Los Angeles county alone, between 1884 and 1888, sixty-two today have no existence.

It was at the end of this boom that the last of four children, the subject of our biography, was born in the Fuller home,

Charles Edward, weighing thirteen pounds—a prophecy of a man six feet, two inches, built for college football, abundantly endowed with the strength and vitality which he was to sorely need for the great burdens that God would later place upon his shoulders.

The mother, increasingly suffering from asthma, hearing that the air about Redlands brought relief to many others similarly afflicted, on a day when she felt she could not stand it any longer, took a train to Redlands, where at once almost all the distress disappeared. In 1889, the father visited friends in Redlands, and was so impressed with the climate and the glorious panorama of the San Bernardino Valley, that he determined someday he would reside there. It was a frosty morning when three miles southwest of the town he went out to look at some property, with the view to purchasing it, and found, on what is called the Bench, a lovely hillside, sunflowers blooming, untouched by the previous frost. Here, he said, would be the place to plant a grove. He first purchased twenty acres, and soon after, fifty more, and began setting out orange trees, sometimes working when the thermometer registered 110 degrees in the shade. He still kept his furniture business in Los Angeles. Always a lover of travel, he attended the great World's Fair in Chicago in 1893, at which time he purchased and sent back to California twenty-seven carloads of furniture, bought from the hotels and rooming houses adjacent to the fair grounds, empty when the fair closed. Soon after this, he moved his family to Redlands, and there he lived for the next thirty years, one of its most distinguished citizens, identified with every worthy civic movement.

Inasmuch as Charles grew up near Redlands, a word must be said about this community into which he was brought when three and one-half years old. Redlands is in San Bernardino County, and during the early history of that area, San Bernardino, fifty miles east of Los Angeles, was the dominating community. The first party of Europeans to see this valley was under the leadership of two priests, Fathers Garas and Diaz, who arrived there March 21, 1774, leading an expedition sent out by the Viceroy of Mexico to open a road between Sonora, Mexico, and Monterey. Garas returned the following year and devoted a good deal of time to exploration in this vicinity, with the result that in 1781 the famous San Bernardino Mission was established. This was destroyed by a revolt of the Indians. A new missionary body of priests was sent out in 1810 under Father Dumetz, and arrived at the site May 20, 1810. This being the feast day of San Bernardino of Siena, they gave the name Bernardino to this area, which it still retains. The earthquakes of 1812 led the Indians to believe that these missionaries were demon-possessed, and they massacred the missionaries and converts living in the mission, and destroyed the buildings. A new chapel was erected in 1822, but raided and destroyed nine years later, rebuilt in 1834, but destroyed again. The decree of secularization of 1832 was now being carried out, and the mission was never rebuilt. Cattle barons now ruled this area. From 1851 to 1858, the old mission grounds were occupied by the Mormons. Under the rule of Bishop Tenney, twelve thousand devotees of the new cult soon came into this area. They paid seventy-seven thousand dollars for San Bernardino Rancho, and there built a fort, which was never used, said to be "the most elaborate fortification ever attempted in Southern California." On April 26, 1853, San Bernardino County was segregated from Los Angeles County.

Telegraph wires first reached Los Angeles in 1861, but were not completed to this city, soon to be a great railroad center, until September 18, 1873. Two stage coach lines each week started from this city to Los Angeles, on Monday and Thursday mornings at seven o'clock, asking eight dollars a passenger for the trip. The city was connected with a railroad, with an assessed valuation of nearly two million dollars. In 1904, the population had grown to over nine thousand, with an assessed valuation of over six million dollars. Some of the most beautiful homes and elegant hotels of all Southern California were built at Redlands, many of which are still standing.

Henry Fuller became a member of the First Methodist Church, which some years before had begun its existence in the old Y.M.C.A. the year Charles Fuller was born, October 16, 1887, with a congregation of forty-three. The church was organized the next month, with a membership of fourteen. In 1890, a church building was erected at the southwest corner of Citrus Avenue and Cajon Street at a cost of (would it not be wonderful if we could build today at such a figure?) fifty-four hundred dollars. Within a year, the membership had increased to 220, by 1898 to 425, and by 1900 to 550, which meant that a new building was necessary. This was erected on the northeast corner of Cajon Street and Olive Avenue in 1901, at a cost, including the property, of about fifty thousand dollars—one of the most beautiful churches in that part of Southern California, with an auditorium seating eighteen hundred people. Here a remarkable Epworth League was established under the ministry of the Rev. B. C. Cory, which by 1904 had a membership of nearly two hundred. The church had an amazing number of activities. There were special courses of lectures, addresses by distinguished authors, illustrated programs of travel, Bible study classes, and classes for the study of missions; in fact, the Methodist Church even began to hold street meetings in 1893, a feature that was continued regularly for many years. At the age of twelve, in 1899, Charles united with this church, but, as he himself says, he had no experience of regeneration, and joining the church really meant nothing to him. Henry Fuller became deeply interested in missions and missionaries, probably from the activity of the church of which he was a member, and at one time was supporting in full or in part fifty-five missionaries and Christian workers.

Father Fuller was built on a California scale, a large man, with great driving power for work. He believed in work, all day, six days a week, and sometimes part of the night. Everyone who was associated with him was expected to give his uttermost to the task at hand, but he would never let anyone surpass him in the hours devoted to labor. He was indifferent to luxury, careless of dress, and very careful in regard to business matters. Theirs was a large, beautifully furnished home, outstanding even in those days of great houses. More than this, Mr. Fuller was a devout Christian. He did not have many advantages of higher education, but he believed the Bible, was a devoted churchman, and was a power everywhere for Christian ideals. The father communicated to the son his great physical vigor, his transparent honesty, his business integrity, habits of thrift, and a reverence for the rights of others. Henry Fuller represented everything that was wholesome and good in those pioneer days of California, without its coarseness, and the fever of risking all one's life and earnings on some wild speculative venture.

Four sons adorned the Fuller home. Harry Ephraim, to whom the father gave the lower twenty acres of his famous orange grove, did not have the father's habits of thrift, and it was necessary for the father to subsequently take back what could have been the means of an excellent income. However, he found his niche later in being the representative in Kansas City of the California Citrus Growers Association. Percy Edmund became a successful lawyer in Los Angeles, and passed away some years ago. Leslie Elmer, born five years before Charles, was the first member of the family to break into *Who's Who in America*, in his middle forties, becoming a professor in Garrett Biblical Institute and Northwestern

University at the age of thirty-one, but meeting sudden death in 1936 in an accident while on a camping and fishing trip in Alaska. Charles was looked upon as the least promising of the four boys. The father confidently believed, at least in the earlier years of his growing family, that Charles would become the least known of any of his sons, and attain the least success. Not that Charles was inclined to carelessness or lawlessness, but he did not have a strong inclination for studies, was shy, and retiring—just one of that type of manhood which does not come into its own until middle life, and whose subsequent career would amaze many who knew him in the earlier days.

The home in which these boys were growing up was one in which, while the father was the head according to the New Testament ideal, it was the mother who took full charge of bringing up this family. The father seldom gave personal attention to his sons. He never played with them, seldom joked with them, and never tried to be on intimate terms with them. The mother was a saint who knew how to keep peace in the home, to iron out difficulties that might arise, faithful to a husband who at times might be difficult, and bringing her boys to the throne of grace every day in prayer for God's blessing, guidance, and protection.

Mr. Henry Fuller in 1902, departing from Redlands on the 15th of July, with his son Leslie Elmer, took what was at that time a most unusual trip around the world, visiting not only Great Britain and the principal countries of the continent, but Russia, Palestine, Egypt, and then China, Japan, India, and Ceylon, sailing for home from Glasgow on the steamship *Astoria*. While on this tour, he wrote a long series of letters for the Redlands *Daily Review,* and upon his return, had the letters published in a volume of some 341 pages, with 42 full-page photograph illustrations, under the title, *A Californian Circling the Globe* (Nazarene Publishing Co., Los Angeles,

1904). On the way east, he stopped in Peru, and attended the church in which he was brought up as a boy, and found only twelve people in attendance, the minister blaming the rainy weather for the small attendance. Certain statements in this volume clearly reveal Mr. Fuller's own prophetic convictions, and also his great passion for missions. He speaks of Jerusalem as "an exceptional city, the central one of Bible history and prophecy, destined to yet play an important part in the world's history, even as in the past." How thrilled he would be to see such hopes as these now coming into remarkable fulfillment. Later he writes, "As often as I call to mind the last time I gazed around from Olivet, I think of what those two angels said, dressed in white and looking like men, as recorded in the first chapter of the Acts of the Apostles. I was not there nearly nineteen hundred years ago to see a cloud receive Jesus Christ as He was carried into heaven, but someday, according to what these two angels said, He will come back in the same way, and I shall see Him (I Thes. 4:16,17)."

While in India, he observed such poverty, degradation, and the emptiness of paganism as he had not seen elsewhere, which led him to say, "The real cause and want of greater success in missions is in so-called Christian lands. The man or woman in England or America that gives a few dimes to missions and one hundred dollars to build and adorn some costly home church that never prays for a foreign mission, that breathes a sigh of relief when the missionary collection is raised, knows of and cares but little for missionary work. With the scanty funds with which missionaries are provided, I think they are accomplishing real miracles."

The great power in the Fuller home when Charles was a boy was the mother, a large woman of Dutch origin, with dark brown eyes, radiating kindliness, in her early days, before marriage, a schoolteacher in the state of New York, highly educated, with great musical gifts. Though a maid was always employed in the home, she did much of her own cooking, loved pretty dishes, and saw that everything in the household was always spick and span. Family prayers were held every morning. The father would read the Scriptures, and the mother would play the organ, while all the members of the family would participate in singing. The father had no social graces whatever, would sometimes be abrupt. The mother's spiritual attainments, confidence in the Word of God, and love for music were all to reappear in greater maturity in the boy Charles, whom the mother loved so dearly, and whose cause she so often championed. Daily she interceded for him at the throne of grace; as the quiet, thoughtful boy went in and out, to school, to play or work, little did she dream that the day would come when her son's voice would be heard around the world, pleading with men to accept Christ.

CHAPTER III

FROM BOYHOOD THROUGH COLLEGE

Dr. Fuller is one who is not given to living over the past. His interest, thought, and concern are for the task of today, the greater task of tomorrow, and the still greater work of another year. Maintaining this habit throughout his life, he finds it difficult to recall interesting incidents of grammar and high school days. He can clearly remember, however, being a Y.M.C.A. cadet, and marching on all great civic occasions. Between the close of a high school year and the opening of a new term in the fall, he would work in his father's orange groves—and work it was. Professor Louis B. Avery became principal of the high school in 1895, and made it "one of the strongest high schools in the state of California." At the time Charles attended there were about two hundred and eighty pupils enrolled, with ten teachers. The fourteen-year-old boy saw President McKinley when he visited Redlands on May 7, 1901, and was with the great throng that welcomed President Theodore Roosevelt when he came through the town May 7, 1903. There were two distinguished teachers in his high school, Mr. Avery in physics and chemistry, and Mr. Hiram Hercules Owen in history (nicknamed by the students H_2O) who dropped into his young heart some ideals for scholarship and reading. While Charles himself was never a scholar, he was a good student, and later, when God called him to found a theological seminary, he insisted that the school have the very highest scholastic ideals. He was exceedingly shy in school. Conversational chatter was

FROM BOYHOOD THROUGH COLLEGE 43

then and has always been something in which he never felt at ease. Sports attracted him, but most social activities he shunned. What happened in his young heart in those formative years probably no one will know this side of heaven. Every boy has his heartaches, his hours of excitement as great vistas of thought and action in the history of the past, in the classics of literature and the developments of science and economics of the present hour, are opened out to him. What influence his teachers and fellow students in high school had upon him, it would be difficult to say. No doubt, as with others so with him, the conversation at the table, words dropped by others at work, the sentences falling from the lips of his teachers, sermons heard on the Lord's Day in church, the faithfulness of some Sunday School teacher, a page from one book, and another page from another, choral groups in which he sang, Y.M.C.A. groups of which he was a member, all played some part in the development of the man whom God was to use for the first great world-wide preaching of the gospel over the radio. With this brief and necessarily inadequate notice of those early days, we must now accompany the eighteen-year-old son of a well-to-do orange grower to the gates of a comparatively new but firmly established college not far from his home.

There was probably not to be found anywhere in America in the years in which Charles E. Fuller was in college, 1906–1910, a more idyllic place for academic life, nothing quite so above the ordinary things of this earth, as the atmosphere that hung over, and the life that was lived in Pomona College, California.

Wherever intelligent people, with deep convictions have moved into new territory, their minds within a few years turn to the subject not only of education, but of higher education. Twenty years after the landing of the Mayflower, Harvard College had its beginning; Charles G. Finney was persuaded in his own mind when he went to Ohio that such a school as Oberlin must be established. So also in Claremont where a college of the very highest academic standards was begun within fifteen years after the first residence had been built. Those who will be reading this book, unacquainted with Pomona College, always a small school (by determination of the Board of Trustees), should not entertain the idea that its comparative smallness might in any way be a criterion for measuring its academic standards. Probably in no small college on the entire Pacific Coast, at the close of the nineteenth century and the beginning of the twentieth, were there gathered together such a notable group of teachers as here. There were men with doctorate degrees from Harvard, Yale, Johns Hopkins, and the University of Pennsylvania, some who had studied in the very best universities of Germany, and others with degrees from Oxford, Athens, and Rome. Professor Frank Parkhurst Brackett, the founder and director of Brackett Observatory, in the autumn of 1911 accompanied Dr. C. G. Abbott, director of the Astrophysical Observatory of the Smithsonian Institute, in an astronomical expedition to Algeria—so high was his reputation in American astronomical circles. Professor Charles Baker, of the Department of Zoology, in co-operation with his colleague, Professor Cook, established what was to become a famous biological institution on the Pacific Coast, the Laguna Beach Laboratory. Professor Edwin Clarence Norton, Dean of the college from 1893 to 1914, had done work in the classics at Yale, Johns Hopkins, Oxford, and Athens, and brought to Pomona College a contagious love for Greek literature and for the highest intellectual ideals. While Charles Fuller was a student at Pomona, publication began of the *Pomona College Journal of Entomology,* and soon after there issued from this small but select school the *Pomona College Journal of Economic Botany,* and the publications of the Astronomical Society of

FROM BOYHOOD THROUGH COLLEGE   45

Pomona College. Dr. Cyrus Grandison Baldwin, President from 1891–1897, who had worked with Professor E. A. Park at Andover Seminary, on the famous conservative theological quarterly, *Bibliotheca Sacra,* often taught classes at Pomona in Christian evidences. Music was given a large place in the collegiate curriculum, and beautiful concerts could be often heard in the college chapel and auditorium.

Many of those who were prominent in Pomona College in those days had direct missionary connections. On the Board of Trustees was the Rev. James T. Ford, graduate of Andover, who, after some missionary work in Vermont, became for some years the Congregational Home Missions Superintendent of Southern California. Dr. James H. Harwood, graduate of Union Theological Seminary, had worked for some years with Dwight L. Moody in Chicago, and later became Superintendent of Missions of the great Southwest. Professor Arthur D. Bissell, of the Department of Germanic Languages, was born of missionary parents in India, while the Rev. Henry Kingman, who became pastor of the College Church in 1900, had once been a missionary in China. On the college seal were inscribed the words, "Our tribute to Christian civilization." Also on the Board at this time was Dr. Walter B. Hinson, then of San Diego, later acquiring fame as one of the greatest Baptist preachers of the Pacific Coast. The president during Charles Fuller's years at Pomona was Dr. George A. Gates, graduate of Dartmouth-Andover Seminary, with graduate studies in German universities, and, before coming to Pomona, president of Iowa College in Grinnell, Iowa.

Charles Fuller was nicknamed "Chub" in high school, a name that went with him into college. Some men begin college with a flash, pick up all the freshmen honors, attract attention from faculty and students alike, and then, toward the end of their four years strangely fade out. But those whose characters are strong and deep, who wear well with their college friends, often acquire their honors toward the end. Charles began playing football as a freshman. By the time he came to his senior year, he was varsity captain. He was also given the highest honor that any school can confer upon a man—president of his senior class, and also president of the Lyceum Debating Society. His most difficult area of study in college was in the field of linguistics. German and French were very hard; even English was not a subject he reveled in. However, in mathematics and science he received such high grades that he could graduate *cum laude*. While majoring in chemistry, he had attained such facility in laboratory work that during the last year he was an assistant to the professor of chemistry, Dr. James Alexander Lyman. This is a load for any college student—studies, debating, football, presidency of the senior class, assisting in the laboratory. He has been a load-carrying man ever since. The issue of the college annual, *Metete,* in the year in which Charles graduated, had inscribed under a picture of him in the back of the book, "Mastodon, largest specimen on the coast," but in the group of class pictures, a more sober part of any college annual, were these lines, "Physically the biggest man in school, mentally a fine student, morally every inch a man."

There was one inner tragedy, however, which was seldom spoken of at the time, but which exercised a great deal of influence over this young man's life in the early days after graduation. While Charles had been brought up in an evangelical home, and had been taught to believe that the Bible was the Word of God, his studies in biology, especially the theory of evolution, had silently undermined his faith as it has undermined the faith of literally millions of other young men. If evolution taught at Pomona could work such havoc with the faith of a young man brought up in an evangelical home, one can imagine what the teaching of

CHARLES E. FULLER
At nine months At four and a half
A boy of fourteen Graduating from college
As a young pastor

FROM BOYHOOD THROUGH COLLEGE

evolution in many of our pagan universities today can do to young men who know nothing of the Word of God—it builds an iron fort around their hearts which is almost impervious to the gospel message. Charles' absorption with science persuaded him to sidetrack the department of English Bible; he went through college growing in a knowledge of the things of the world, but not growing in a knowledge of the Christian faith. Only a radical experience of conversion, brought about by the use of the Word of God, by the Holy Spirit, through an anointed servant, and by his mother's prayers, delivered this young man from the dark cloud of unbelief which had settled down upon his heart. But that is still a few years away.

While Charles was at college, his father had invested a large sum of money—large for today, very large for those days—in a gold mine, near Forest Hill, on the south fork of the American River, north of Sacramento, not far from where gold was discovered. He insisted that his son start his postcollege career by supervising these mines, or at least watching over them and working in them. We cannot speak of the gold mine experience without a word concerning the whole gold mine industry of California.

"In 1839, a Munchausen-like character, who had ambitions to become a feudal baron on the frontier, John A. Sutter, after a dubious career in several parts of the world, deposited on the shores of California, by the simple expedient of fabricating a glamorous European past, secured both recommendations and credit." So vividly does the latest narrator of the gold-mining industry of California, Dr. Rodman W. Paul of Yale University, describe this famous character. On the Sacramento River, where the city of Sacramento now stands, he built a famous fort, New Helvetia, and established there a tiny empire over which he ruled as dictator. He contracted with James W. Marshall, a mill-wright and carpenter, for the construction of a mill on the American River, forty miles from the little kingdom of New Helvetia. Marshall built a diversion dam, and because of this, on January 24, 1848, one of his helpers wrote in his diary: "This day some kind of metal was found in the tailrace that looks like gold, first discovered by James Martial, the Boss of the mill." By one test and another that night and the next day, Sutter and Marshall knew that what they had found was gold. News traveled slowly then, but within three months the rush was on, such as the western world had never seen, and will never see again; in fact, on the 29th of May that year, the San Francisco *Californian* felt compelled to suspend publication, complaining, "The whole country, from San Francisco to Los Angeles, and from the sea shore to the base of the Sierra Nevadas, resounds with the sordid cry of 'gold, Gold, GOLD!' while the field is left half planted, the house half built, and everything neglected but the manufacture of shovels and pickaxes." In 1848, California produced a little less than a quarter of a million dollars in gold; in the next year that had risen to ten million, and in 1852, the figure had risen to eighty-one million dollars. It slowly declined, until in the 70's, it averaged around seventeen million dollars. However, out of California in the last century over three hundred million dollars worth of gold has been mined.

The gold rush days were over, of course, when Charles Fuller just out of college, went north to Forest Hill, a town twenty-five miles from the railroad, the final four miles a narrow trail down a steep rocky canyon, but many of the factors of the early days were still predominating. It was a rough life, food was poor, accommodations were primitive, the type of men employed were of a very low order, while profanity, drunkenness and wickedness of every type made camp life a sordid affair. What a change—from the almost heavenly atmosphere of Pomona to the brutality, coarseness, and materialism of a gold mining camp, and yet all within the same state. Mining gold does not make for golden character. Henry Fuller's mine was what was called a "dredger" gold mine. A huge dredger machine, on a raft or boat was set out in the middle of the river, where dredges would bring up from the river bottom, which could not be reached by ordinary mining processes, tons upon tons of sand and gravel. The wet mass would be dropped into funnel sieves, where powerful streams of water would separate the small particles from the larger stones. The stones and larger pieces of gravel would be carried off, and the finer gravel would drop through onto a belt to be carried into a crock, where, by what was called the mercury process—which, by the way, was known far back in Pliny's time—the gold would be separated from the worthless sand. This was an expensive process, and unless the area mined showed a fairly high gold percentage, there was either no money in it for the owner, or a loss. It was the latter that marked Henry Fuller's venture, and here, like many others, he dropped a small fortune, something over one hundred thousand dollars.

Charles stayed here for almost a year, lonely, disappointed, shocked to discover a life so utterly different from that in which he had grown up. Most of all, he was far away from the one he loved. While at the camp, Charles had an accident, when pulling himself across the fast-flowing river in a boat. The current was swifter than he had expected, and more powerful than he was able to contend with, and the boat was suddenly swept out from under him, the powerful current whipping him about. Convinced he was not going to be able to hold on to an overhanging rope until a rescuer should appear, he uttered a prayer to God, like Jonah of old in the belly of the great fish, and told the Lord that if He would spare him and save him from death, he would serve Him the rest of his life. But like many similar promises made by men, and sometimes by women, in hours of great peril or threatened death, the vow meant little, and Charles soon forgot what he had told the Lord. The Lord did not forget. He had need for this young man, though the young man knew it not, and the day would come when he would not only serve the Lord, but would render a service that would bring the name of His Saviour to millions who otherwise might not hear of Christ.

Almost bewildered, certainly convinced that this was not the kind of work in which he wanted to spend his life, he returned home and finally persuaded his father that the mine could not become profitable. The father suggested he come back to Redlands and work in his orange groves. This is exactly what Charles wanted, and for the next few years he will be identified with the flourishing, fascinating orange industry of Southern California.

CHAPTER IV

IN THE ORANGE GROVES

Oranges, for some strange reason, are not mentioned anywhere in the Bible, though most of the outstanding Biblical episodes took place in what could be called the citrus belt of the Mediterranean. Grapes, figs, and olives grow where oranges grow, and though the three here first named are often mentioned in the Scriptures, oranges never are, even though in earlier days some thought that Leviticus 23:30 might refer to the golden fruit—"And ye shall take you on the first day the fruit of goodly trees, branches of palmtrees, and boughs of thick trees, and willows of the brook; and ye shall rejoice before Jehovah your God seven days." The word here translated *goodly trees* is the Hebrew word *chadar,* which earlier students thought must refer to the citron, a view that is now given up. Incidentally, however, while oranges are not mentioned in the Bible, and probably were not growing at that time in the Near East, today seventy thousand acres of the Holy Land are devoted to orange groves, and something over fifteen million boxes of oranges a year are shipped from Palestine to various parts of the world. Inasmuch as Dr. Fuller's earlier years were spent in this ever increasingly complicated work, a word here concerning the orange industry is, I think, not out of place, for millions of people in our country who hear the Old Fashioned Revival Hour, while frequently partaking of oranges, have never seen them grow.

There is probably not a more beautiful sight in the whole world of horticulture than an orange grove in fruit. The trees themselves are spherical or conical in shape, depending upon the way they are trimmed. The leaves are a deep green and glossy, and are found in thick masses so that very little sunlight can penetrate a full-grown tree. These trees grow from fifteen to forty feet in height, and are planted between twenty and thirty feet apart; a Valencia grove will generally have seventy trees to an acre, which, in a good season, might yield seven hundred boxes of oranges. No trees are more carefully tended than those of the orange groves of Southern California. Every tree is watched over with minute care. The fruit hangs singly, and, when ripe, may measure anywhere from an inch and a half to eight inches in diameter—golden balls hanging from the top of the tree to the lowest limb, framed in a background of tropical green. In the blossoming season, the odor of the orange trees is so strong that it permeates the entire citrus region, giving off a perfume such as no other fruit trees known to man exhale. As gold is the so-called king of all metals, desired by men from the dawn of history, so oranges are rightly called the golden fruit, for they are indeed the king of all fruits, and those growing them somehow are looked upon as the aristocrats of any community.

Oranges may grow generally to within thirty-five degrees on either side of the equator, but the fruit is thought to have originated in Asia, some records, if they are dependable, indicating that oranges were known in China as far back as 2000 B.C. No citrus species is native to America, the first citrus seed having been brought to Haiti by Columbus, November 22, 1493, reaching continental America in July, 1518, in what is now called Guatemala. Within the next thirty years oranges were planted in Florida, and two centuries later wild citrus groves were still to be seen in that southern peninsula. It was not until 1769 that the first orange seedlings were planted in California, the first orange grove being set out in the famous San Gabriel Mission in 1804, not far from the city of Los Angeles. Some of these trees were still in existence at the turn of the twentieth century. Seedlings were planted in the Los Angeles area in 1834, and in less than thirty-five years, there were seventeen thousand orange trees for commercial purposes bearing fruit in Southern California, of which fifteen thousand were in the Los Angeles area. As Los Angeles itself, however, began to grow, and orange groves were given up for building purposes, Riverside became the center of the orange industry, and by 1880 there were as many orange trees near Riverside alone as in the entire state of California thirteen years earlier. Today California has something over three hundred thousand acres planted in orange trees, and produces eighty million boxes of citrus fruit annually.

There are two kinds of oranges grown in Southern California, the Valencia, which bears fruit from April to September, and the Washington Navel, which bears fruit from November to April. Recognizing that oranges, if in sound shape and weather conditions are favorable, can be kept on the trees for nearly two months after they have grown to maturity, one can see that it is possible for oranges to be picked in Southern California in almost any month of the year. The Valencia orange—and it was with this type exclusively that Charles Fuller worked—was first introduced into Southern California in 1876, just eleven years before he was born, by A. B. Chapman and George H. Smith, who, strangely, received an unlabeled package of orange trees from a famous nursery in England. The variety, when planted, produced fruit late in the season, so that Chapman called this new orange the Rivers Late, but at a subsequent time a citrus grower from Valencia, Spain, identified the variety as one grown in his native country, and Chapman was persuaded to call the orange the Valencia Late, which name it has carried ever since. It has now been introduced into practically every citrus area of the world, and, says our greatest authority on oranges, "is unquestionably the most important late-maturing variety grown. It is more extensively grown than any other orange in California, Florida, Texas, and South Africa, and is doubtless grown more widely and on a larger acreage than any other citrus variety in the world."

For the growing of oranges California has strong advantages, and equally strong disadvantages. The California orange does have a delightful flavor, and a very high color, which makes it more easily marketable. It has a long holding capacity on the trees, and the climate of California makes it possible to extend the harvest season over long periods. On the other hand, California is a long way from the great markets of America. Land is very expensive in Southern California, some orange groves having been sold from time to time at a price as high as five hundred dollars an acre. Labor also is not to be had cheaply. California's greatest problem is water. All orange groves in Southern California are irrigated, and this irrigation must be practiced for periods of forty-eight hours every three weeks. Here also, as in Florida, there is the danger of a freeze. Whenever the temperature drops to freezing, 32° F., orange groves are at least in danger, and often the temperature does drop below freezing in January and February. To offset this, a great system of smudge pots has been developed, one pot being placed adjacent to every tree in the grove. These smudge pots burn oil, and when a whole valley is threatened with low temperatures, one wakens in the morning to see the entire sky black from the fumes of these small stoves. Smudge pots can raise the temperature of the air about seven degrees, and oranges can stand temperatures as low as 27° F., if such does not prevail for too long a time; consequently, most orange growers can still keep their fruit when the temperature goes down as low as 20 °F., but below that there is no hope. When at night one hears government reporters announcing possible temperatures for any particular area, say at two o'clock in the morning, and figures are given below 20°, as we heard this last winter, he knows that the fruit is gone in that area, for the most part, unless the orchard is located on a hillside, or where there is an unusually favorable atmospheric condition. Beyond all this, the orchardist—as all fruit growers in America know, must fight increasingly powerful armies of enemies, insects, parasites, fungi, worms, and all kinds of strange diseases that threaten to blight a tree. The orange may be called the golden fruit, and an orange grower may be looked upon as the aristocrat of his community, but no man in America has such a constant struggle to bring his fruit to maturity as the orange growers of California.

While oranges by nature are given in their thick skin a natural protection for the fruit within, an orange nevertheless, strange to say, is very easily bruised, and when a bruise does take place, blue mold soon generally sets in, which will of course ruin the fruit for marketing. Before the actual picking of the fruit from the trees takes place, a so-called "picker" goes through the orchards, nipping the stems of the fruit about to be plucked with a pair of clippers close to the fruit itself, so that when the orange is taken from the branch, no hard protrusion is left which might scratch the other oranges. After being taken to the packing house, oranges generally stand for a day or two, during which time some of the moisture in the rind evaporates, making the skin a little tougher for handling. The fruit is soaked in deep trays of warm water, and then passes through long rows of revolving brushes, which wash away any particles of dirt. It is then rinsed in cool water, and passed under a blast of air, where it is dried. On the canvas belt, trained women sort the oranges into grades, according to size and appearance. There are ten principal sizes of oranges, from 100 to 344, that is, 100 to a box to 344 to a box. In some packing houses the crates are cooled before placed in iced cars, or, in the winter time, of course these cars are heated. No fruit-growing industry in the world is as highly organized as the citrus growing industry of Southern California. So complete is this organization, and so binding its laws, that no orange grower will pick without orders from the central association to which he belongs. If there is a glut in the market, picking is reduced to a minimum. If the price is high, the amount picked is raised to a maximum. All orange growers in any one vicinity are allowed to pick the same proportion of fruit to their total crop in any one given time, so that no orange grower can flood the market with his entire crop in one week. The crop is sold in a pool, and proceeds are divided among the orange growers according to the quality of the fruit they have raised, and the quantity their respective orchards produce in any one season.

During summer vacations in boyhood days, Charles would work in the groves, but by the time he had reached the age of sixteen, six feet two inches in height, with a strong, vigorous body, broad shoulders, and developing muscles, he was capable of hard work, and hard work was what his father believed in. He was entrusted with no responsibilities, just laboring, often with foreign laborers, and he loathed it. After graduating from college and when his gold-mine experience was over, he devoted his time entirely to the packing end of the orange industry. With a team of horses, he would haul the fruit from the grove itself, perhaps two or three miles from the packing shed, would dump it into a contrivance called a "dumper," from which the oranges would flow out into a belt, where they were graded, the father devoting himself for the most part to this important process of grading. In addition to hauling the fruit, he was the box rustler of the plant. When a box of oranges in the packing shed had been fully packed, he would pick it up and carry it to the presser, where a cover was placed on it and automatically clamped down with metal. From the packing table he would carry the boxes into the box car at the side of the packing shed. Oranges must be stacked with great care or the fruit is bruised. The tiers were six boxes high, and if a

IN THE ORANGE GROVES

man was not tall, with strong muscles, when he came to the sixth tier he would have to do a lot of pushing, and would be inclined to simply drop the box. Charles could stack these tiers as no one in the packing shed. There was no time for loafing in the way that packing oranges was carried on in those days. It was work, and more work. Sometimes they would begin before the sun was fully up, and often they would work into the night. Some of his days were eighteen hours long, and so tired was Charles when night would come that he would drop into bed, too weary to even eat. Before he knew it, another long day was beginning. There are a great many men today, successful men in our country, who, fifty years ago and more knew such long, strenuous days of hard work, and it did not seem to result in any notable harm. Today men do not break down from overwork, as a rule, but from the tensions of life, from frustration, from the high speed of industry, from worry over huge organizational and financial loads, and, taking all kinds of opiates and stimulants, they are robbed of normal sleep and rest, only to enter upon the second half-century of their lives close to the border of nervous prostration, or some coronary trouble. There were no automobiles in those days, night life was frowned upon in Redlands, and those participating in it were socially shunned. Drunkenness among the better classes was almost unheard of. And so the Lord, unknown to this young man, was developing him physically, and preparing him for the years of business ahead in growing and packing oranges, which would usher him into the great radio ministry which God knew was to be his life work, though radio itself had not begun to be developed in the days when Charles was rustling boxes in the Redlands packing plant. Hardships and crushing reverses were to come to him in this very strange industry, before the call of the Lord led to the beginning of the Old Fashioned Revival Hour.

Chapter V

MRS. GRACE PAYTON FULLER

We must now pick up the second most important theme of our story—the beloved companion, helpmeet, and tower of strength for Charles E. Fuller during these thirty years of his ministry, his beloved wife, Grace Payton Fuller. To properly appraise the story, we should go back a little ways into another pioneering episode in American history, the settlement of what is called the Great Northwest, or the Oregon Country, which in the early days embraced the states now known as Oregon, Washington, Idaho, the western half of British Columbia, and the extreme western portions of Montana and Wyoming, an area approximately one-fifth the size of the entire United States. It was a land of great contrasts, with mighty rivers, large lakes, lofty mountains, beautiful valleys, a great variety of soil, climate and fauna and flora. In fact, as a recent writer has said, "there is in the Pacific Northwest something no other part of America possesses in quite the same degree: a freshness and promise as though the future had not quite run out of the hourglass, as one so often feels it has along the Eastern seaboard and in the Old South, and even in many parts of the Middle West. This feeling has been packed into two enticing and nostalgic phrases: 'the Last Frontier, the Last Evergreen Playground.'"

This vast area, in which had been living, for how long no man knows, at least 125 different tribes of Indians, was probably not seen by any white man—Sir Francis Drake had not sailed that far north—until Sebastian Vizcaino in 1602 reached Oregon, and left such place names as Cape Blancho and San Sebastian. Then nearly two centuries passed, 170 years, and two years before the signing of the Declaration of Independence another "alien eye was laid upon that roaring coastline." Spain then began to compete with Russia for the full trade of the Northwest, a story which, however fascinating, cannot be entered upon here. In 1792, when George Washington had been President of the United States for three years, and when the population of the then United States had nearly reached four million, was the Columbia River seen for the first time by a white man, Robert Gray, a Boston fur trader. Just after the turn of the century, one of the most famous expeditions of early American history was undertaken by Captains Lewis and Clark, which aroused interest of Americans in the Oregon country, and led quickly to an expansion of the American fur trade in that area. Among other places which they explored was the Willamette River Basin, located in what is now northern Oregon, rising in the mountains near Eugene and flowing north 125 miles until it enters the Columbia River between Portland and Vancouver, from whence it flows into the Pacific Ocean. Because we are more interested in the Willamette Valley than in any other part of the northwest, a description of it, written in the early 60's may be of some interest. "The Willamette River and Valley, fifty miles wide, is the garden of Oregon, the holder of nearly two-thirds of all the inhabitants of the state, the chief source of its present strength and prosperity, and its sure security for the future, lifting it above the uncertainties of mining, and giving guarantee of stability, intelligence, and comfort of its people. Though this valley now supports a population of fifty thousand by agriculture only, probably not one-tenth of its area has yet felt the plow. Its best lands can be bought from five to twenty-five dollars an acre." The source of the Willamette River was discovered by two Clarks in 1812, which aroused interest, especially for fur traders, in the wealth of wild game in this territory.

As the "Oregon fever" took hold of many of pioneer boldness in the East, the Methodist, Presbyterian, and later, Episcopalian denominations were led to attempt the establishment of missions in this rugged, sparsely-cultivated land. In fact, even as early as 1798, before the Lewis and Clark expedition, a German, Baron August von Schrinding, proposed to the London Missionary Society a program for Christian pioneer work in this area, but the plan was never carried out. At Andover Theological Seminary in 1810 and 1811, another project was being formulated, and, at the same time, the American Board of Commissioners for Foreign Missions, representing the Presbyterian, Congregational, and Dutch Reformed denominations, were beginning to direct attention to the Oregon country. However, it was by the Methodist Missionary Society a few years later that definite mission work was finally established here. A letter written to the *Christian Advocate and Journal* of New York City, March 1, 1833, aroused tremendous interest in the East in the need for Christian work in the Oregon country. The story is one of the most fascinating in American history. It told of four Nez Percé and Flathead Indians who made a journey over land to St. Louis, and visited the home of General William Clark, then Superintendent of Indian Affairs, saying that they had heard of a new way of life and of a book that had come from God, and they would like someone to come out to their people and tell them what God wanted men to do as recorded in that book. Two of these Indians died while in St. Louis, and were given a Catholic burial, a third is thought to have died on the return trip, while the fourth safely returned to his people. Out of this came the bold, sacrificial pioneer work of James

Lee and Daniel Lee, New Englanders of a long line, who arrived in the Oregon country September 15, 1834, warmly welcomed by the dominating personality of that whole area for years, Dr. John McLaughlin, called by the Indians, the Great White Eagle.

Year after year, with unflagging zeal, hundreds, and soon thousands, struck the Oregon trail for their westward home, a new hope, and, for some, a fortune. The movement of 1843 became known as the Great Migration, when 875 men and women were added to the population of the Willamette Valley alone, raising the total population of that area to 1500. Two years later, the total population rose to six thousand, and in 1849, over nine thousand people, by a careful census, were living in the Oregon territory, nearly all of whom were American citizens. Seymour Dunbar, in his fascinating work, *A History of Travel in America,* reminds us that "not far from two million square miles of territory were penetrated and occupied as a direct or indirect result of the overland hegiras that took place in America between 1840 and 1850 . . . the most extensive area of the earth involved in any similar phenomenon within a like interval of recorded human history."

In none of the great waves of immigration to the west was there a more substantial group of people than those who were to be seen slowly wending their way toward the Pacific on the Oregon trail. "Down-and-outers found no place of welcome in Oregon caravans. A considerable outlay of hard-earned cash was needed before going over the trail, to outfit one's self with essential equipment—wagon, livestock, foodstuffs, tools. The people of the dependable classes were to constitute the bulk of home builders, settlers, and trades people throughout the Willamette-Puget trough, and in southern Oregon. From their ranks, many originally from New England, came the political, educational, and moral leadership." Most of these caravans started from Missouri about the first of May, when the streams were fordable, and grass would be adequate for their animals. They traveled on an average of ten miles a day, and therefore reached the Willamette Valley before the rainy season set in in October. Each family had one covered wagon in which, in addition to the driver, the women and children, with all their belongings, including a plow, seed, bedding, food, were carried. There were no cushions and springs such as we know. Anyone who has ridden in one of these relics in our own day finds one mile all he cares to endure. They were hardy people who could take this for four months straight.

For the most part, these pioneers were Christians, far more than any other group settling up to the middle of the nineteenth century on the whole Pacific coast. Moreover, being people of high intelligence, many of them college graduates, they early determined to establish adequate educational institutions. At the town of Willamette, as early as 1844, the Oregon Institute was opened, October 13, to receive its first five students, before its first building had even been completed— the third educational institution to be established in the Oregon country. Within a score of years, it was to change its name to the Willamette University, and a historian of its notable career rightly said that around Willamette University "are gathered the histories of all the years since Methodism brought civilization and Christianity together to the shores of the Pacific." The most notable member of the faculty of its early days was Joseph Wythe, a Methodist clergyman who arrived at the university in October, 1865, to begin his career as President of Willamette University, who, says a recent historian of medical education in the northwest, was "probably the first who had a considerable equipment of scientific and medical training to be placed in a position of educational responsibility in the state. He belongs to the category of the sturdy group who felled forests, built roads and bridges, and attempted to bring law and order into the wilderness which others had discovered. He was the teacher, and organizer, and builder of institutions and character." It was Wythe who in 1851 issued the first in America, and one of the first in the English language, of many books on the microscope, *The Microscopist, or A Complete Manual on the Use of the Microscope,* a work which passed through four editions by 1880. With Wythe bringing his enthusiasm for medicine to Willamette, it can be easily understood that this university must, sooner or later, have a medical school. By action of the Board in 1865, Willamette announced the Medical School of its now famous university. This great medical school, the third to be founded west of St. Louis was "in point of continuous existence, until it closed its doors in 1913, the oldest from the time of first organization. In 1867, Willamette had a population of 4500, exceeded in Oregon only by the city of Portland, the university enjoying an enrollment of over 250 students.

It was in the spring of 1862 that Dr. Daniel Payton, who had been practicing for some years in Keokuk, Iowa, started out with his beautiful wife, Elizabeth, and two children, to follow the Oregon trail, by oxteam, in a covered wagon, a journey that even then entailed many hardships. Not a day could be lost if they were to arrive at their destination before winter should set in. On the way, a baby was born that lived but a few hours, necessitating its immediate burial, and the trampling down of the little grave by all the covered wagons in the caravan, so that the Indians would not be aware that a body had been buried and dig it up. On the trip, the frail wife contracted tuberculosis, and though she lived for fifteen more years, and gave birth to several more children, she never enjoyed robust health. The Payton family settled near Salem, where Dr. Payton immediately opened an office and began the practice of medicine, which he continued for nearly thirty years. During this time, he served as Dean of the Medical School of Willamette University, and when in 1878, he felt called upon to retire from active teaching work in this department, the Board of Trustees passed the following resolution of appreciation: "Dr. Payton was one of the principal founders of the Medical Department of this university. During its entire history he has held in it a professorship, and for two years was Dean of the faculty, and during all these years the Medical School and the university has had no friend more devoted, more faithful, and more useful than he. The valuable services he has rendered have often been given at a personal sacrifice."

The most famous of Dr. Daniel Payton's children was his son, John Eberley, born in Keokuk, Iowa, June 9, 1857, and thus five years old when the trek to Oregon was undertaken. He graduated from Willamette University and then took his medical degree there, while his father was serving as Dean. At the very early age of eighteen, in July, 1875, the future doctor married Eliza Kinney, the seventeen-year-old daughter of Robert Kinney, who many years before, in 1847, had himself crossed the plains from Iowa, with his wife, Eliza Lee Biglow, arriving in Oregon in the autumn of 1847. In the years that followed, Mr. Kinney developed a large and lucrative lumber business, and became a man, for those days, of considerable wealth. The log cabin which they quickly erected when coming into Oregon in 1847 was soon exchanged for a large, commodious house. Mr. Kinney, when hearing of the discovery of gold, rode horseback to San Francisco, and after an absence of nearly two years, returned with a chest of gold containing ten thousand dollars! Not all men pursuing gold came back with such a large sum. In addition to the lumber business, he shipped sheep to South America, and started the first flour mill in Oregon. His daughters were educated in a convent, the only day pupils allowed in that institution. Two of his own sons went to New York for medical training at Bellevue Hospital, returning after the railroad was completed in 1872. One of them, Dr. Alfred Kinney, was twice president of the Oregon State Medical Association, once when a young man, and again fifty years later. The father was a devout man, with all of his vast business enterprises, and also a great reader: his three most beloved books, copies of which were bound in black oilcloth, were the Bible, Shakespeare, and Blackstone's Commentaries on the Law.

Medical practice in Oregon was not too lucrative, even when extensive, in those early days. Grace, daughter of Dr. John E. Payton, later to be the dearly beloved wife of Charles Fuller, was born in Drain, Oregon while her father was acquiring fame as one of the outstanding doctors of that area. She recalls that "Nine months in the year, the climate was bad, with heavy rains and deep snow. The roads were poor, often only trails. My father rode horseback while he made many of his calls, carrying his drugs, bandages, and dry socks in saddle bags, and the horse he rode was often required to swim swollen rivers. Many a time he reached home soaked to the skin, and weary, having stayed all night to see some woman through a hard case of child labor, or to help as he could until a desperately ill person had breathed his last. I recall his telling how differently people faced their last hours on earth: a fine Christian would die victoriously and praying, some even glimpsing heaven or singing, as his own mother, Elizabeth, did in her last hour, softly whispering in song, 'What can wash away my sins, nothing but the blood of Jesus.' One terrible experience which my father never forgot was seeing an atheist die, cursing God, 'if there was one.' He received little money for his treating the sick, but rather took in pay whatever the people had to give—apples, sheep, hams, oats—most of which he disposed of for cash. His very first case in moving to Drain was a woman who had typhoid fever, and was sick nearly all of the summer, coming very close to death. My father made many trips to see her, riding ten miles in each direction on every visit, week after week, sometimes almost every day, staying hours in the home at the time of crisis. When she had recovered, the husband, a blacksmith, said, 'Dr. John, we sure appreciate your pulling Mama through this sick spell. It's surely been a long pull, and a hard one. I cannot pay you, but I'll tell you what I will do, I will make you a nice pair of andirons, a poker, and a shovel for your fireplace.' My father was disappointed, for he was trying to save enough money to go to the Polyclinic Hospital in New York for post-graduate work, and he had hoped for a fairly good fee. However, those very andirons have been used all these seventy-five years, first in Eugene, Oregon, then in Redlands, California, and now they hold the logs for the cheery fires in our little winter home on Smoke Tree Ranch in Palm Springs." Grace Payton, the faithful companion for these many years of Dr. Charles E. Fuller, was born into this doctor's home ten years after her father had there begun his practice.

The Payton family, father, mother, and daughter Grace, went to New York City when the little one was four years old, that Dr. Payton might take some special work in the New York Polyclinic Hospital. On a walk one chilly day in near-by Central Park, Grace developed a severe case of diphtheria, and in those days any type of diphtheria was a terrible thing to face. For days her life was despaired of, but God graciously restored her, and when she had sufficiently recovered, the family returned to Oregon.

After a brief sojourn as a doctor in Eugene, Oregon, and another short period in San Jose, California, where he planted a cherry orchard, in anticipation of giving up the practice of medicine because of increasing ill health, Dr. Payton moved, with his wife and daughter, in 1895, to Redlands, California. Here again he built up a large practice, fortunately for others specializing in tuberculosis; for at that time Redlands was becoming famous as a health resort, noted for its wonderful climate, and hundreds of men and women suffering from this scourge came from all over America to seek relief from a disease which in those days was not handled with the efficiency and hope of recovery that now generally attend it. Mrs. Payton herself tirelessly served on the Board of the Associated Charities, and Dr. Payton was for years a faithful member of the Board of Trustees of the First Baptist Church.

Two children were now living in Redlands who were, even in high school days, to fall in love with each other, and who, in the councils of God, were some day, as Dr. and Mrs. Charles E. Fuller, to send out the gospel through the air every Sunday to millions listening at their radios. Although the Payton and Fuller families were, of course, known to each other, both enjoying positions of outstanding importance in this city of orange groves, and although both entered the same high school in the same year, 1902, it was not until toward the junior year that, as far as they can remember, they were introduced to each other, Charles being the bashful boy rushing around to find a cap, which he might use in a graceful bow, when his chum told him he wanted to introduce him to "a very nice girl." Something clicked, in that mysterious way that love has, one of the sweetest mysteries of life—and let it remain a mystery—when this sixteen-year-old boy, without social graces, but athletically inclined, with a countenance of wholesomeness, revealing a character that could be trusted, looked into the face of this beautiful girl; and that moment he thought, as he has continued to think for now nearly a half century, that here was for him the one and only girl in the world. Even close friendship however, did not immediately develop. Other young men were drawn to her, as naturally they would be, one of them being the very Beau Brummell of her group. As often happens, there apparently was growing up in both of their hearts a real affection for each other, which neither expressed to the other, until what normally would have been a trivial incident, without any notable consequences, proved a turning point in both of their lives.

When the father, Henry Fuller, returned from his remarkable world tour, he brought with him trunks full of curios—fans, oriental rugs, silk garments, ivory objects—all of which were arranged on long tables in the great Fuller home, allowing friends to come in and see these tokens of an orient which at that time was visited by so few in our country. Three girls, including Grace Payton, made arrangements to drive out the four miles to the Fuller home to see this museum of objects from the other side of the world. The weather being warm, according to the custom in those days Grace carried a fan. After spending some time looking over these beautiful products of ancient cultures and civilizations, she discovered when they were about to leave that her fan had disappeared. The mother of the Fuller home promised that if it were found she would send it over to the Payton house. The following Sunday, when Grace answered the ringing doorbell, the six-feet-two friend of high school was standing there with the fan in his hand. Mrs. Fuller insists today that Charles purposely stole the fan while she was at the Fuller home, hoping that out of this episode there might arise an opportunity for some definite meeting with the one he was secretly coming to love, but Charles denies this—we can all have our own opinion about it. This was the beginning of regular Sunday afternoon visits. The Fuller family went to the Methodist church in the morning, as the Payton family went to the Baptist, but on Sunday afternoon young Charles drove back to Redlands from the Fuller ranch, spent a few hours in walks, talks, and drives, filled apparently, as have the walks and talks of so many been filled, with sweet nothings which meant everything, stayed for supper, and then together they went to the young people's service and the evening preaching service. In their senior year, both graduating from high school in 1906, Charles, normally so timid, driven by this most powerful of all emotions by which the world revolves, asked Grace if she would marry him. Wisely, she told him she could not give an answer then, they were too young, let time tell if their love would last through the vicissitudes and the changes which college would inevitably bring to both of them.

While Charles entered Pomona College, which we have written about in a previous chapter, Grace went to the Cumnock School of Expression, founded by Robert McClain Cumnock, the distinguished professor of Northwestern University, who there had founded and presided over for more than a quarter-century the famous Cumnock School of Oratory. After reaching sixty years of age and moving to Southern California, he established this new School of Expression, and there Grace studied dramatics, especially Shakespearian dramatics, English, with emphasis upon diction, public speaking, and French. As Charles engaged eagerly in debating while at Pomona, and his future wife received training in a similar subject, in which she had remarkable gifts, both were, wholly unknown to themselves, being prepared of God for their great public oral ministries a score of years away.

The following year, 1907–1908, Grace Payton enrolled as a student at Western College for Women in Oxford, Ohio, a town named for Oxford, England, located one hour's ride from Cincinnati, in the beautiful rolling country of southern Ohio, a school which had opened in 1855, under the name of the Western Female Seminary. The President when Grace attended was Dean Mary Alma Sawyer, though between 1908 and 1912, Dr. John Grant Newman served as president, later one of the most beloved Presbyterian ministers of Philadelphia. Western College for Women, today one of the outstanding women's colleges in America, always emphasized the great truths of the Christian faith, and the pre-eminent value of a life ruled by the will of God. It is interesting to note that Western College today has one of the most noteworthy schools for radio speech and radio programs of all the smaller colleges of America (though, of course, radio was simply unheard of when Grace was a student there). During all this time, a regular correspondence was carried on—two letters each week from Oxford to Pomona, and two from Pomona to Oxford. Probably the number two was not always rigidly adhered to; under such circumstances, the necessity for writing more frequently very often mysteriously arises. Through such letters, sometimes young people come to know each other better than when in each other's actual company, at socials, driving, walking, or reading together.

Returning home after the first year at Oxford, Grace and Charles saw a great deal of each other throughout the summer, and before September had closed, they were engaged. My English professor once told me he thought it was a criminal intrusion upon the sacred precincts of life for the love letters of Elizabeth Barrett and Robert Browning ever to have been published. He may have been right. Into all the sacred meaning of their engagement we have no intention of intruding here. One must remark however, before we see the young people part again for their respective schools, that Grace was a girl of great beauty, a beauty which in spite of long spells of illness that were to follow, of tireless work for the Lord, and the unshirked burdens of a household, she still retains—lovely brown hair, black and flashing eyes, a countenance of infinite sweetness, a personality that radiates that something which no instrument of science has yet been invented for measuring, what we call charm, loveliness, abounding energy, clothed in womanly grace and refinement.

Instead of returning to Western College for Women, in the fall Grace went to the University of Chicago, where William Rainy Harper was still reigning as one of the great college presidents of America, and where were gathered together at that time probably the most notable band of professors that could be found in any university in America, outside of Harvard and Yale, and perhaps including both of them. There had developed however in the University of Chicago a spirit of criticism of evangelical Christianity which later on was to rest as a blight upon the Divinity School of that institution, and to rob thousands of young men of faith in the saving work of Jesus Christ, the Son of God. Near-by was a famous Unitarian church, where a gifted orator was the regular preacher, and due to her love for dramatics and elegant diction, Grace regularly attended the Sunday morning service when this man was in the pulpit. Before the year was out, her faith in the great verities of the Christian religion was practically gone. This has happened over and over again in our country. I can remember some years ago in a town where I was pastor, the daughter of the Superintendent of Schools, himself a godly man and superintendent of a great Sunday School, went off to Columbia University for graduate work in education, and in eight months came back declaring she did not even believe in God—a position she still maintains. I have even seen young men with a passion for evangelism enter some of these schools whose professors deny the deity and resurrection of Christ, and the inspiration of the Scriptures, and within two years are not only bereft of their evangelistic passion, but convinced there was nothing for them in the Christian ministry—a judgment awaits those professors who have crushed the faith of young men in our day. The tragedy with most of them is that they never come back to God. With Grace Payton it would be different, by His infinite love, for, though returning home a Unitarian, she would yet experience a supernatural regeneration by the power of the Holy Spirit and be delivered of that which, had it remained sovereign in her heart, would have prevented her from ever going before a microphone with a message of comfort, of salvation, of forgiveness, and of hope through Jesus Christ for sinners. Before the year was out, Dr. Payton was taken seriously ill, passing away in May, 1909, a change in circumstances at home which persuaded the daughter not to continue her university work, but to remain with her widowed mother, Grace being the only child of the family. Charles was still at Pomona, to graduate in the spring of the following year, and often came down by train to Redlands, twenty-five miles away, to visit the one he adored.

After his wretched year spent in the gold mines, of which we have already spoken, Charles, at his father's request, returned to Redlands to work in the orange groves, which brought him back to the city in which his loved one was living. At the home of her mother, on the evening of October 21, 1911, Grace Payton and Charles E. Fuller were united in marriage, and to this day, thirty-eight years later, Charles and Grace Fuller have been in love only with each other. Those who have been in the Fuller home, and have heard him speak to Grace, and heard her speak to or of him, and have seen them together under all kinds of circumstances, on joyous occasions and in hours of great crisis, do not have to be told how deep their love for each other is. Some distinguished people think it is necessary once a year, or more often, to get away from each other for a few weeks, or a month or two, one taking a boat to Europe, while the other stays home, or one running off to visit with the mother while

The Home of Dr. and Mrs. Fuller in San Marino

the other goes in an opposite direction to visit someone else. All this may have its place in the lives of some, but not for the Fullers. The only time they are absent from each other is when either sickness, business, or the Lord's work has made it necessary. Everywhere this husband goes, he wants his wife with him, and though she has great independence in her own actions and decisions, nothing of any importance is ever determined in that home except one consults the other and both are agreed. I do not think on the printed page for the public to read one should record too many of the gracious and lovely intimacies that one observes in being in their home or with them on various occasions, but I cannot help but speak of one. I have more than once accompanied Dr. Fuller from the front door of our home to his car, where his dear wife might be sitting, reading or writing out some material for the broadcast, and have heard him say, "Isn't it wonderful to be married to someone as beautiful and lovely as my wife?"—and this from one who has celebrated his thirty-eighth wedding anniversary.

Chapter VI

THE GREAT CHANGE—CONVERSION

In the early days, when the Fullers were still living at Redlands, there came to that city from the east a frail woman afflicted with tuberculosis by the name of Mrs. Leonora Barnhill. Though she had been a school teacher for some years, she found it necessary before resuming her teaching work to take some special courses, and to support herself by working in a novelty store, where the day was eleven hours long and the pay was five dollars a week. At different times, she lived in the home of Dr. and Mrs. Payton, and the daughter Grace soon began to recognize the remarkable Christian character of this woman, and listened attentively to everything she had to say. It so happened that this little woman was consumed with a great love for the Lord Jesus, and a desire to make Him known to all she met. When Grace Payton returned from a year at the University of Chicago in the summer of 1909, she rather boastfully declared to her now widowed mother, and to Mrs. Barnhill, that she felt a Unitarian view was about the broadest and smartest form of faith that one could accept, namely, that one worships only God and takes Christ as a mere example for daily living, looking upon Him as a noble teacher and a most loving individual, but not one who was divine or to be acknowledged as the Son of God. Mrs. Barnhill, in her gracious, quiet way, looked at the young lady, and said, "Grace, Christ said, No man cometh unto the Father but by me, and, my dear, you have no way of approach to a holy God unless you come through Christ his

THE GREAT CHANGE—CONVERSION 75

Son as your Savior." Mrs. Fuller said later, "The Scripture which she quoted was the sword of the Spirit, and at that moment Unitarianism was forever dead in my heart. I believed that moment, though I said nothing, and believing God's Word, I instantly became a new creature in Christ."

Is it not true that most people whom God greatly uses have had a real, definite experience of conversion, a *radical* conversion? I am sure there are some in the Christian church greatly used of God who do not know the day when that took place, though they are thoroughly saved. But what one fears today is so many of our young people just growing up in the church, hearing sermons, even listening to the Bible taught in Bible classes, participating in young people's summer conferences and the like, without knowing what it is to pass from death into life, and to have a new life within them, which is communicated only by the Holy Spirit of God. Men like Wesley, Moody, Mel Trotter, Billy Sunday, R. A. Torrey, and Gypsy Smith all had this vital, definite revolutionizing experience of regeneration. This is what came that evening to Grace Payton, and this is what would soon come to the one she was to marry, Charles E. Fuller.

We must for a moment move on from Redlands to Placentia, where the Fuller home is established, and record one of the visits of this saintly woman, now for some years in glory. She brought with her a small book, by the outstanding teacher of the Plymouth Brethren assemblies in America in the nineteenth century, F. W. Grant, whose writings have had such a great influence upon many Bible scholars in the last three generations. The volume, not too well known today, was *The Mysteries of the Kingdom of Heaven,* a small, paper-covered book of less than eighty pages. Mrs. Fuller read the book at once, and was so deeply impressed with it that she pleaded with her husband to give a few hours to reading it himself. Now Charles Fuller was not at that time reading religious books, nor interested in religious matters, but he did acquiesce in the request of the one whom he so greatly loved, and sat down one evening to read what he thought would be a rather dull affair. To the contrary, he became fascinated with it: God used the volume to sow the seed of the living Word in his heart, which was soon to become effectual in bringing forth an experience, of being born again by the Word of God.

I have read the book through myself recently, and was (incidentally) surprised, for one thing, to discover how much emphasis was placed here on infant baptism. Mr. Grant probably got this from his earlier years in the Church of England, which he served in Canada. Today the book seems a little dull. There are, however, a few subjects in this book which later were to enter vitally into the oral ministry of Dr. Fuller, truths re-emphasized and enlarged upon for him when later he became a student of Dr. Torrey at the Bible Institute of Los Angeles. I would mention three of them: In regard to the tares and the wheat, Mr. Grant says, "Meanwhile, tares and wheat *do* grow together. The dishonor done to Christ in Christendom no means of ours can ever efface or rectify. No, not even the most zealous preaching of the gospel, however blessed the result of that, will ever turn the tares of Unitarianism, Universalism, annihilationism, popery, and what not, into good wheat for God's granary. Nor can we escape their being numbered with us as Christians in the common profession of the day. If we meet them at the Lord's table, as if it were no matter, or we could not help it, we should proclaim ourselves 'one bread, one body' with them (I Cor. 10:17); for 'we, being many, are one bread and one body; for we are all partakers of that one bread.' But while refusing to link ourselves with them to the dishonour of our Lord and Master, we cannot put ourselves outside the common profession of Christianity to avoid companionship with them

THE GREAT CHANGE—CONVERSION

there. Nor if we had power, have we skill to separate infallibly the Lord's people, many of them mixed up with most of the various forms of error. 'The Lord knoweth them that are His' is alone our comfort. He will make no mistake. And 'Behold, the Lord cometh,' is the only available remedy which faith looks for, for the state of things at large."

A few pages later, Mr. Grant departs from a close attention to the thirteenth chapter of Matthew, and, taking up for a moment the famous passage in II Thessalonians on the coming of the man of sin, he says, "The passage in the Thessalonians exhibits, however, the 'man of sin' as the distinct head and leader of the latter-day apostasy, and, moreover, declares to us how far this apostasy shall extend. The coming of the 'wicked one' is declared to be with a terrible power of delusion which will carry away captive the masses of the unconverted among professing Christians until none of that middle or neutral class remain. 'Whose coming is after the working of Satan, with all power and signs and lying wonders, and with all deceivableness of unrighteousness in them that perish; because they received not the love of the truth, that they might be saved. And for this cause God shall send them *strong delusion, that they may believe a lie,* that *they all* might be damned who believed not the truth, but had pleasure in unrighteousness' (vv. 9–12). Thus terribly shall close the history of Christendom. The true saints once taken out of it, the door of grace will be closed forever upon those who have rejected grace. They will be given over to become, as they speedily will become, from being *un*believers of the truth, believers of a lie. The wheat being gathered out of the field, tares alone will be found in it." These truths among others were in the years to come to go forth over the air to millions of listeners.

What made the greatest impression, however, upon Mrs. Fuller, and what led her to commend the book to her husband, was the passage almost at the end, concerning the work of Israel in world redemption at the end of this age. Whether or not we would agree with every statement of Mr. Grant is not the point here, but the passage was important in the later thinking of Mr. Fuller, and I take the privilege of quoting it: "But after the saints of the present time have been caught up to the Lord, and Christendom has become a tare-field simply, a new work of the Lord will begin in Israel and among the surrounding nations, to gather out a people for *earthly* blessing. It is when God's judgments are upon the earth the inhabitants of the world will learn righteousness. And this will be a time of 'great tribulation,' such as for Israel Matthew 24 depicts. Antichrist is there, and the 'abomination of desolation' stands in the holy place; yet amid all the evil and sorrow of the time the 'everlasting gospel' goes forth (Rev. 14:6,7) with its call, so opposite to the proclamation of this day of grace *now* being made. 'Fear God, and give glory to Him, *for the hour of His judgment is come.*' "

Another spiritual influence was being exerted upon the Fuller family—a Bible class held every week by one of the most distinguished physicians of Orange County, Dr. H. A. Johnson, who had come down from Canada at the beginning of our century, seeking relief from, if not a cure for a condition of tuberculosis, a graduate of Toronto University, and of the University of California. About 1910, Dr. Johnson began teaching a Bible class in his own home at Anaheim on Thursday evenings, but the class soon grew so large that they had to move into rooms at the First Presbyterian Church, when the time for meeting was changed to Saturday night. After five years of a Saturday night class, the church requested that it become a regular part of the Sunday School, and for thirty more years Dr. Johnson taught the class on Sunday morning, when week after week, year after year, there would be an average of one hundred and twenty-five people attend-

THE GREAT CHANGE—CONVERSION

ing. This skillful physician was equally gifted in unfolding the Word of God. He would expound one book at a time, and during those years, nearly the entire Bible was covered, some books being taught more than once, such as the Gospel of Matthew, the Epistle to the Ephesians, and the Book of Revelation. Here the young wife, Mrs. Grace Fuller, received not only a knowledge of the Word of God, but a love for it, which has never departed. But the husband, having no interest in spiritual things, like any natural man without the Holy Spirit in his heart—a daily reaffirmation of the statement of Paul to the church at Corinth, that the things of God are only foolishness to an unregenerate man—would drive his wife to Anaheim, four miles from Placentia, and while she was listening to the Word of God, he would attend some movie theater.

After the removal of the Fullers to Placentia, Mrs. Barnhill continued to regularly visit the home, where she was always welcome, not only by Mrs. Fuller, with whom she had such close fellowship in spiritual things, but by Mr. Fuller himself, who always found her conversation edifying and indeed instructive. As Mrs. Fuller has said recently of Mrs. Barnhill, "She had much charm, a sense of humor, an unusual understanding of human nature, and a great love for people. I loved her dearly, and Charles enjoyed her visits. She had a fine mind, read widely, discussed almost any subject intelligently, but her outstanding characteristic was Christian love. She lived the life. Her Bible was her constant companion."

The Fullers had looked forward to having a family of five or six children, and when they had been living in Placentia for about a year they were delighted to know they might soon expect a little one in their home. But Mrs. Fuller was not well; the baby did not live; and the disappointed mother developed tuberculosis. The next three years she spent on a screened porch, in bed most of the time with three additional years before sound health returned. Those were years of great devotion on Charles' part, and of great spiritual growth for the one so weak. In the summer of 1917, she with her mother and a friend, went to Big Bear Lake, hoping that the change of climate might bring about a restoration of health and vigor. Such separations were always hard for these two young people so utterly devoted to each other. On Sundays especially the young husband was exceedingly lonesome. He had no interest in church, and generally spent the day reading the Sunday paper, polishing the car, and just loafing around, as hundreds of thousands of men are in the habit of doing in the western world on Sunday.

However, one Saturday while the beloved wife was at Big Bear, Charles read in an afternoon Los Angeles newspaper that one he had known in college days as an amateur wrestler and boxer was to preach in the Church of the Open Door, that great institution where Dr. Torrey was pastor for many years, one of the most important Protestant churches on the entire Pacific Coast, with its vast auditorium seating some thirty-eight hundred people. The man announced was the famous evangelist, Paul Rader, at that time pastor of the Moody Memorial Church, Chicago. Charles Fuller determined that evening that whatever else would happen, he was going up to Los Angeles on Sunday afternoon and hear this former prize fighter. In 1917, Paul Rader was thirty-eight years old, built like a giant, made of iron, with a passion for souls, a rich experience of grace, and one of the great preachers of the saving work of Christ on the North American continent. His preaching laid hold of the hearts of men. The Holy Spirit used his words as arrows, and thousands of souls were pierced with divine truth, a conviction of sin, and a desire for Christ under his ministry. All over America today one still finds men and women who were saved through Paul Rader's preaching, or who came into a new experience of rededication and consecration. Little did Charles Fuller know when he entered

THE GREAT CHANGE—CONVERSION

that building that afternoon what a powerful message would flow from the lips of this man whom he came to hear out of mere curiosity. He probably had never heard any sermon in all his life delivered with such power of the Holy Spirit as what he was going to hear then. Entering the building he found the auditorium crowded—he could find only one vacant seat, behind a pillar, a pillar he can identify to this day. Mr. Rader preached that afternoon on the words from Ephesians 1:18, "The eyes of your understanding being enlightened, that you may know what is the hope of his calling, and what the riches of the glory of his inheritance in the saints." He had not been preaching many minutes before the Holy Spirit began to do a work in the heart of this young man who had come into that building so complacently, expecting that the afternoon would be a little different from most of the Sunday afternoons he had spent previously, but never dreaming his whole life would be revolutionized that afternoon; for without what happened that afternoon, Charles Fuller the evangelist would have had no existence.

One does not, as a rule, describe one man's experience, especially a deep, searching experience of heart, with words which another man has written about his similar experience, but there comes to my mind in this hour an autobiographical parallel, written some years ago, concerning a similar hour under the preaching of the greatest evangelist of the nineteenth century, D. L. Moody. I refer to an experience of Arthur Christopher Benson, son of the Archbishop of Canterbury, one of the most distinguished of modern English essayists, who, in his now seldom seen book, *The House of Quiet*, tells what happened to him when as a brilliant student at Cambridge University, he went to hear Mr. Moody preach: "My life had become almost purely selfish. I was not very ambitious of academical honours, though I meant to secure a modest first-class; but I was intensely eager for both social and literary distinction, and submitted myself to the full to the dreamful beauty of my surroundings, and the delicious thrill of artistic pleasures. I have often thought how strangely and secretly the crucial moment, the most agonizing crisis of my life, drifted upon me. I say deliberately that, looking back over my forty years of life, no day was so fraught for me with fate, no hour so big with doomful issues, as that day which dawned so simply and sped past with such familiar ease to the destined hour—that moment which waved me, led by sociable curiosity, into the darkness of suffering and agony. A new birth indeed! The current of my days fell, as it were, with suddenness, unexpected, unguessed at, into the weltering gulf of despair; that hour turned me in an instant from a careless boy into a troubled man. And yet how easily it might have been otherwise—no, I dare not say that.

"It had been like any other day. I had been to the dreary morning service, read huskily by a few shivering mortals in the chilly chapel; I had worked, walked in the afternoon with a friend, and we had talked of our plans—all we meant to do and be. After hall, I went to have some coffee in the rooms of a mild and amiable youth, now a church dignitary in the Colonies. I sat, I remember, on a deep sofa, which I afterwards bought and still possess. Our host carelessly said that a great Revivalist was to address a meeting that night. Some one suggested that we should go. I laughingly assented. The meeting was held in a hall in a side street; we went smiling and talking, and took our places in a crowded room.

"In a sweet, powerful voice, with an exquisite simplicity combined with irresistible emotion, an assistant, Ira D. Sankey, sang, 'There were Ninety-and-Nine.' The man was transfigured. A deathly hush came over the room, and I felt my eyes fill with tears. Then the preacher himself—a heavy-looking, commonplace man, with a sturdy figure and no grace of look or gesture—stepped forward. I have no recollection

THE GREAT CHANGE—CONVERSION 83

how he began, but he had not spoken half-a-dozen sentences before I felt as though he and I were alone in the world. The details of that speech have gone from me. After a scathing and indignant invective on sin, he turned to draw a picture of the hollow, drifting life, with feeble, mundane ambitions—utterly selfish, giving no service, making no sacrifice, tasting the moment, gliding feebly down the stream of time to the roaring cataract of death. Every word he said burnt into my soul. He seemed to me to probe the secrets of my innermost heart; to be analysing, as it were, before the Judge of the world, the arid and pitiful constituents of my most secret thought. I did not think I could have heard him out—his words fell on me like the stabs of a knife. Then he made a sudden pause, and in a peroration of incredible dignity and pathos he drew us to the feet of the crucified Saviour, showed us the bleeding hand and the dimmed eye, and the infinite heart behind. 'Just accept Him,' he cried; 'in a moment, in the twinkling of an eye, you may be His—nestling in His arms—with the burden of sin and selfishness resting at His feet.'

"I went out into the night, like one dizzied with a sudden blow. I was joined, I remember, by a tutor of my college, who praised the eloquence of the address, and was surprised to find me so little responsive; but my only idea was to escape and be alone: I felt like a wounded creature, who must crawl into solitude. I went to my room, and after long and agonizing prayers for light, an intolerable weariness fell on me, and I slept."

"Leaning my head on the seat in front of me, I trembled there under deep conviction, though I did not know what was the matter with me," Dr. Fuller wrote in a letter some years later. That hour he was saved.

Charles E. Fuller, thirty years old, son of a well-to-do orange grower, recipient of all the honors which students could confer upon him at college, conscious of real business ability as he superintended one of the great packing houses of Southern California, married to a lovely Christian, walking about in a magnificent body, resisting the gospel, indifferent to the things of God, conscious that something was lacking, but unwilling to confess it to anyone, nor to acknowledge it to himself, standing, as it were, on the threshold of mature life, with the normal temptations, disappointments, recurring restlessness, of any strong man, confronted with the growing mysteries of life, for this man at this hour everything within was so churned up that he almost staggered out of the building with bewilderment. Getting into his car, he drove out to a secluded spot on the circumference of Franklin Park in Hollywood—not then the crowded, flesh-pursuing incarnation of worldliness that was soon to make it so famous throughout the world. There, under some eucalyptus trees, he got into the back of his car, fell down on his knees and gave his life completely to God. Whatever Charles Fuller does, he does thoroughly, with all his might. He has never retreated from the decision and vow of this hour. Doubts were swept away, resistance to God was broken; where darkness was, light now flooded. This big man physically, beloved socially, successful in business, was now a new creature in Christ Jesus, and a life he had never known until this July afternoon surged through his being, rushing in to possess his mind, and heart, and very body for Christ. Little did he know out there at the edge of the park by himself that after some time had elapsed, he, orange grower and packer, ignorant of God's Word, now a child of God, would be used by the Holy Spirit, who had that afternoon given him new life in Christ, to begin the Old Fashioned Revival Hour from a microphone placed in the Women's Club of Hollywood, only a few blocks from this spot.

"I went back to the evening meeting," the letter quoted above continues, "to hear Paul Rader preach another sermon, which seemed to me like manna from heaven. My heart was fairly bursting with joy, and all desire to get ahead in the business world and to make money left me. I just wanted God to use me, if he could, to win souls for Himself."

Life is one thing, and without it, no growth or expression is possible; but if a new-born creature is to bear fruit and be used of God, he must absorb the Word of God into his very life before he can express it with his lips. He must know the testings of life's trying experiences, that he may know what it is to trust God under all conditions, and he must have a heart open to the whispers of the Holy Spirit, that he may know what God wants him to do, and be willing to obey when the command should come. All this, unknown to Charles Fuller, was to be his in the years that followed, leading to another great hour, another great turning point in his life, when the local preacher of Placentia would become a herald of the gospel to which a world-wide audience of millions of men and women and children would listen every recurring Lord's Day. Little also did this young man know that within a few years he would be attending, as a student, the great Bible Institute of Los Angeles, housed in the very buildings in which the Church of the Open Door functioned, and that within fifteen years he would be the President of the Board of Trustees of this Bible Institute, probably the largest at that time on the North American continent, with the single exception of the Moody Bible Institute.

CHAPTER VII

GOD'S QUIET LEADING AT PLACENTIA

The Spirit of God gives different gifts to different men for the edification of the church, for the building up of the body of Christ. He distributes these gifts as He will. By this it is not meant that these gifts are bestowed without recognition of the innate capacities and talents with which one is born, but that, whatever the talents, the Spirit of God directs certain men to do certain types of work: some are apostles; some pastors, some teachers, some evangelists. When the Spirit of God sets apart a man for any one of these holy ministries that individual is aware of such designation. He may be indifferent to the Spirit's leading; he may resist it, as some have done; he may immediately yield himself to the direction of the Spirit of God, whether he is aware or not of the bestowal of any particular gift. This obedience to the Holy Spirit is immediately manifested in a Christian's life when the leading is for full-time Christian service. As soon as Charles Fuller was converted, he felt a powerful urge to begin teaching the Bible, though he knew very little about the Word of God. The wholesome thing is that he knew he knew very little about it, and set about to rectify this lamentable situation, to acquire knowledge where ignorance was so predominant. Here again is the mark of true Divine leading. The tragedy with many who have a profound experience of regeneration and feel called of God to engage in the ministry of the Word is that they immediately rush into Christian service unprepared and unequipped. They look askance at institutions raised up for training ministers of the Word,

GOD'S QUIET LEADING IN PLACENTIA

publicly repudiate theological seminaries and Bible institutes, loudly acclaim that nothing else is needed but "the enduement of the Holy Spirit," and begin carrying on a ministry that must be, for the most part, an appeal to emotions, a ministry of excitement and sensationalism. If ignorance of the Word of God continues, this person is liable to go off on some tangent—divine healing, speaking with tongues, date-setting, or some other dangerous perversion of the truth. All Christians are well acquainted with Paul's classic passage on the inspiration and profitableness of the Word of God, which he wrote to his son in the faith, Timothy, in which he declares that all Scripture is inspired of God, and is profitable for teaching, for conviction, for correction, and instruction in righteousness. However, very few think of the concluding clause of this great sentence, which really gives the ultimate purpose of the Word of God, *"that* the man of God may be perfect, thoroughly furnished unto all good works." A study and knowledge of the Scriptures are to make us fruitful, as Paul elsewhere says, in every good work.

At this time Mr. Fuller had no intention whatever of becoming a minister of the gospel. Apparently the Spirit of God did not reveal the ultimate plan which God had for him, but nevertheless this young man felt he *must* teach the Word of God. Knowing very little about the Word, he spent every spare hour he had apart from his heavy business responsibilities in a personal study of the Holy Scriptures, and began at once to pass on what he was discovering.

Mr. Fuller organized what was called "The Unearthly Hour Bible Class," meeting in the Denominational Church of Placentia. It was given this strange name because the class assembled on Sunday morning at eight o'clock. The teacher literally fed his people on the Word of God. Just as people are by instinct drawn with expectation to a table set with good things, so Christians who love the Lord find themselves irresistibly drawn to that place where the finest of the wheat, the Bread of Life, is being distributed for the nourishment of their souls. This has happened over and over again, in every age, in every nation on earth, where a child of God stands up with the Word of God on his lips, earnestly and intelligently seeking to communicate eternal truth. The class grew amazingly, and soon no room in the church was large enough for the numbers who came, and they found it necessary to move to a building quite unique in its attractiveness for a town the size of Placentia, the Round Table Clubhouse. With larger quarters, the class experienced further growth. News spread throughout Orange County that a young man was opening up the Scriptures and people were finding truths in the Word of God which were meeting their deepest needs. As often has happened in other places, a feeling of jealousy, or a fear that one part of the church would become top-heavy, developed, and the time came when, without previous word to the teacher, in a meeting of the Sunday School officers where he was present, wholly unaware of what was about to be said, Mr. Fuller heard it announced from the floor that an adult Bible class would begin its first session at that church the following Sunday morning. Upon asking before the assembled group if this meant that his own class was no longer to be counted a part of the life of that church, he was told that was what the announcement meant.

This automatic severance with one of the churches of town apparently did not in any way affect the growth and vitality of the Bible class. Many were attending who were not vitally identified with any Protestant church in Orange County. Many more had been saved in the class and were yet without a church home. No split ever occurred from any other church. No group of people was drawn out of a church to establish some rival organization, as has so often happened, frequently with tragedy. But this body of people, trusting their teacher

GOD'S QUIET LEADING IN PLACENTIA   89

and knowing that he was instructing them out of a pure love for the Word of God, undoubtedly exercising a gift from God, urged him to consider the founding of a church. In May, 1925, Mr. Fuller had been ordained by a group of Christian ministers, at Modesto. The movement was so strong, the reasons were so apparent, that Mr. Fuller finally consented. This meant the erection of a building. On October 15, 1925, the cornerstone was laid for this new building at the corner of Bradford and Chapman avenues, directly opposite to and on the east side of the street from the Round Table Clubhouse. The building was planned to cost between twenty-four and twenty-five thousand dollars, but like many other plans for building the figure was too low: the ultimate cost, with a slight addition to the Sunday School, was forty thousand, five hundred dollars. The building was dedicated February 21, 1926, a beautiful, commodious structure to which no picture does full justice. There seems to be a spaciousness about the auditorium that gives one a sense of expansiveness. Twenty classrooms for Sunday School activities are found in the Sunday School addition; a large kitchen, a social hall, and offices for the pastor, a church secretary, and an additional worker were all taken care of in the original plans. Probably some will ask, why a new church? "For some time," said an official announcement, "there has been an urgent need felt and expressed from many sources for a church organization where only and all fundamental doctrines of the Bible are upheld and supported by those wishing to lend their united influence against the worldwide trend toward modernism and materialism. The new church will be interdenominational, fundamental, and evangelistic, the motto being, 'We preach Christ crucified, risen, and coming again.' " In June, even before it was decided to erect a building, eighty members were bound together in ties of mutual fellowship. Two years after the building was erected the Sunday School had a regular attendance of over two hundred. During Mr. Fuller's pastorate, which terminated in 1932, four hundred and ninety members were enrolled, of whom, outside of the original eighty, ninety per cent had united with the church upon confession of faith. Inasmuch as this is probably the only time when the history of this church will be written, at least for some years, it might be well to note the men who were the original officers. As directors the following were elected: Thomas B. Welch, O. W. Lillie, Frederick Armstrong, C. H. Flory, W. E. Peitsch, and Charles E. Fuller. On the Board of Deacons were T. B. Welch, O. W. Lillie, Frederick Armstrong, C. H. Flory, M. M. Loitz, and W. Wallenius. The Board of Trustees elected were as follows: J. F. Prather, Grover Murdick, B. J. Rouse, J. M. Levier, and George Crosby.

At the dedication of the building Dr. Charles Hulburt, founder of the Africa Inland Mission, and a great help to the church in its early days, read the Scripture and gave the opening prayer. Mrs. Robert Harkness, wife of the famous Gospel pianist, sang two of her husband's compositions, and Dr. Louis S. Bauman, gifted minister of the Brethren Church in Long Beach, gave the address of the day on "Labor Is the Supreme Business of the Church of Christ." Dr. W. A. Hillis of the Bible Institute of Los Angeles gave a short message.

The pastor of the church was still engaged in extensive business activities, and took no salary from the church at any time while he was its pastor, but every hour that could be spared he devoted to the study of the Word of God with particular emphasis, it would seem as one looks back over the announced subjects, upon prophetic matters. He often preached a series of sermons on the Book of Revelation, or the Patmos Visions, or on the Book of Daniel, or on Anti-Christ, and on Heaven, and, in addition to Gospel messages setting forth salvation, sermons on revival, on the anointing of the Holy Spirit, etc. Like many of the rest of us when we were young, Dr. Fuller did not hesitate to preach on the subject of evolution. In November, 1927, the announcement read: "Next Sunday Mr. Fuller will speak upon two vital messages, 'Bloodless Religion' and 'Satanic Counterfeits.' Many honest and sincere people are perplexed because of the many kinds of religions today. Can all religions, because there is so much good in them, be from God? Does it make any difference which one you believe in, providing you are true to that one? Does the Bible teach one true religion, and if so, which one? In the Sunday morning message, 'Bloodless Religions,' Mr. Fuller will endeavor to show the falsity of the teachings of Unity, Christian Science, New Thought, Theosophy, Spiritualism, Modern Theology, and Unitarianism. Mr. Fuller's sole purpose in dealing with this subject is to warn and instruct in a kindly way and point out in the light of God's Word that these teachings are not only wrong, but are both subtle and dangerous, and attack the very heart of Christianity, the blood. In the evening message Mr. Fuller will reveal the counterfeits on the Second Coming of Christ, as taught by Christodelphianism, Russellism, Mormonism, Bahaism, or the Universal Religion." No doubt there were people then who would say when they heard these topics announced, "Now why bring up these subjects? Why not just let these sleeping dogs lie? Why drag these subjects of contention into the pulpit?" Well, the years that have elapsed since these subjects were announced have overwhelmingly shown the necessity for warning the people of God about these counterfeits. Christian Science is still growing and in some cities in California the Christian Science church will have the largest audience on Sunday morning of any group in an ecclesiastical edifice. Agents of Mormonism are ringing the doorbells of thousands of people every day, and many young sons and daughters of devout Christian homes are marrying Mormons and abandoning the Protestant Church. Dr. Fuller has never ceased his warning concerning these Satanic cults, and for such he has paid a price straight down through the years, for powerful groups from certain of these organizations have done everything they could to thwart the work he has undertaken as God has revealed tasks for accomplishment.

And what about prophecy? Well, as a paper in Santa Ana once said in commenting on a prophetic message of Mr. Fuller's when he was at Calvary Church, "Either this man is crazy, or what he is saying is of the greatest importance, and he seems to have the Bible on his side." Well, did he? Occasionally, in the late twenties and early thirties, he would speak on the prophetic significance of Russia and the increasing power which it was to wield in these last days. Did he have this right? The truth is today the only powerful nation left on earth (apart from our own, thank God) is Russia. Germany is in ruins; France, a second-rate power; Great Britain's empire has been shaken to the foundations; but this country, Russia, is looming up, as prophetic teachers said it would, in fearful and powerful opposition to everything with which Christ has been identified. One notices that on April 26, 1931, Mr. Fuller preached on "The Rise of the Ten Kingdoms." It is a very strange thing, though perhaps not so strange, certainly unique, that just now leaders in Europe are talking about the "League of the Ten Nations." I have before me a clipping from the New York Times dated May 4, 1949, headed: "Ten Nations Speed Council of Europe," with a subtitle, "Rule of Unanimity to Govern Choice of Topics for Debate in Democratic Parliament."

In addition to faithfully interpreting the Word of God himself, the pastor brought in some of the finest Bible teachers and evangelists in America to his little church. Often there came Dr. Bauman from Long Beach, and Mr. Hillis from Biola. In 1926 Dr. John MacNeil, the famous Scotch evangelist, came to Calvary. In 1928 the church heard the greatest Bible teacher of his day, Dr. G. Campbell Morgan; in 1929 that Baptist warrior of Toronto, T. T. Shields; the evangelist, Paul Rood; the Bible teacher, W. P. White. The following year Harry Von Bruch held a great evangelistic meeting for Mr. Fuller. In 1931, Miss Cristobel Pankhurst, the gifted English speaker and writer on prophecy, came to Calvary Church, as well as Dr. Charles G. Trumbull (of whom we will have more to say later) the brilliant editor of the Sunday School Times of Philadelphia, to hold one of his famous, profoundly moving conferences on Victorious Life. In 1932, Dr. Fuller's last year at Calvary, Mel Trotter came to hold evangelistic meetings, and Robert Glover, Home Director for North America of the China Inland Mission, held a conference on missions. As one looks over the list of speakers, we find some whom, of course, we have not named, that have since lost their message, men who have gone off on tangents, who have eliminated themselves from the great body of believers, or who have fallen into sin and are no longer preaching the gospel which once they declared with power.

A good insight into the happenings at Placentia, and the evangelistic passion which everyone was seeing in this young minister is revealed in a letter received from the well-known evangelist, Dr. Harry O. Anderson, at whose wedding Dr. Fuller was best man, and with whose two sons Dan Fuller attended high school:

"My first contact with Dr. Charles E. Fuller was the receipt of a letter asking if I would come to Orange County in a county-wide C.E. series of evangelistic meetings. I think it was in 1922 at the opening of my evangelistic career. I motored down from my home in Oakland, California, in my Ford, taking two days to make the trip, arriving a very tired man in the evening preceding the meetings. I reported to the home of Mr. Fuller at Placentia on their orange grove. Assisted in the meetings by E. Raymond Couch, consecrated song leader who could play the ukulele and whistle the sweet gospel melodies, we covered the churches of Orange County. Dr. Fuller who was a faithful Bible teacher and gifted in the ministry of teaching seemed to receive an evangelistic urge from this campaign that prepared him in a measure for the great evangelistic emphasis of his entire ministry. I was early impressed at this consecrated football captain of Pomona College, now operating a large orange grove, but on fire for the things of Christ. The fellowship in their home was like the Psalmist says, 'Our fellowship was sweet.'

"Our second campaign was in the form of a Tabernacle that was erected in Placentia adjoining the property where the Placentia Church was to be erected and carry on a gracious ministry. It was an event for one church and individual to erect a portable tabernacle to attract the attention of the people to the gospel. Assisting in this campaign were Rev. William E. Pietsch, now of radio fame at Waterloo, Iowa, and Rev. Hugh P. Andrews, Portland, Oregon, giving their special talents and attention to the music and the young people. To attract the interest of the people we announced the ascension of a large red, white, and blue balloon as big as an average garage. Attached to the balloon was an announcement of the meetings and a reward for returning the slip to the Tabernacle meetings. A great crowd gathered, the balloon fired up, a sponge wet with fuel was placed underneath the ascending balloon, and up she went and almost out of sight. It was a dry, sultry day. Somehow Andrews and others were impressed to follow it in their cars and fortunately for all concerned, for it landed on the roof of a dry barn and would have burned the entire structure if someone

GOD'S QUIET LEADING IN PLACENTIA

did not get on the roof and pull it off, extinguishing the blaze before any amount of damage was done. Fuller, Anderson and all felt God was in that impulse to follow the balloon for it would have worked great difficulty and hindrance to the meetings if the barn was destroyed. Incidentally that form of advertising the gospel has never been used since. From these meetings a great evangelistic spirit was developed and, if I remember correctly, came at the opening of Dr. Fuller's broadcasting experience at Santa Ana.

"Our third effort was at the completion of the Placentia Church, a beautiful and well-equipped structure dedicated to Bible teaching and evangelism. Harry D. Clarke was the song leader. Mrs. Harry D. Clarke and Mrs. Harry O. Anderson assisted in those meetings. Dr. Charles E. Fuller was the pastor at that time and carried on his radio ministry through the Santa Ana station. No doubt God was preparing him here for the great world-wide ministry that was to follow. Incidentally, Mr. and Mrs. Charles E. Fuller made a very generous gift at this meeting which made possible the purchase of a portable tabernacle that could be shipped all over California and the United States for the large number of city-wide union meetings that I was privileged to conduct. Thus in a very vital way, they have a share in every ministry that won countless numbers to Christ.

"We recall vividly when Dr. Fuller travelled in the interest of the Gideon work and came to Oakland and in a large, cold, modernistic church, gave his simple testimony and urged the support of Bible distribution by the Gideons; thus he was faithful in the small place as well as in the larger ministry that came later." One cannot help but inserting something here of a lighter vein.

In the middle of Dr. Fuller's ministry it was announced that a certain evangelist of the Middle West was coming to California for a Sunday morning service. The announcement reads: "This is an unexpected and unusual opportunity to hear one of America's greatest evangelists. Dr. —— is said to be the greatest speaker since William Jennings Bryan. He is termed the 'Billy Sunday of the East,' and where he goes great crowds come to hear him." The author of this book, when he came upon this name, knew that as far as he was concerned he had never even heard of the man, which was a little extraordinary, inasmuch as this was the "greatest speaker since William Jennings Bryan." He ought to have been heard of. So the author asked Dr. Fuller himself who he was, and he said he could not even remember the man. He has asked some others; no one can remember his coming and no one can even recall who he was. This is a lesson we all need—not to speak of men beyond that which they deserve, and not to write advertising copy for ourselves which later will only cause laughter.

Not only did Dr. Fuller bring in the very best Bible teachers and evangelists available in this country, but he himself frequently was away speaking at famous conferences. From the very beginning he would often go down to the Sherman Institute at Riverside, where two thousand Indians were being educated, and preach the Gospel to these men, driving back again for his evening services. As early as 1925 he was speaking twice a day at the annual Southwest Bible Missionary Conference in Williams, Arizona, taking with him his friend of many years, of whom we will speak again shortly, Mr. Leland Green, with his saxophone. In 1927 he was speaking at conferences held by the Bible Institute of Los Angeles, at Walla Walla, Washington, and Ocean Beach, California. In 1928 he was back again at Walla Walla, and Touchet, and later speaking, twice a day, to two hundred and fifty pastors at a convention in Macpherson, Kansas, and later, for a whole week, every morning at the vast Cadle Tabernacle in Indianapolis.

GOD'S QUIET LEADING IN PLACENTIA

A church takes both its tone and tempo from the shepherd of the flock. Mr. Fuller was endowed by God with inexhaustible resources of energy, and when he was converted God gave to him as a prime asset in his Christian life the pre-eminent passion to get the Gospel out to the unsaved. It does not take a congregation long to know what its pastor thinks the chief interests of his ministry, nor is it long before sensitive Christians partake of the passion that possesses the one from whom they are receiving the Word of God. From the very beginning Calvary Church, Placentia, was throbbing with evangelistic fervor. First of all, its members became keenly interested in missions. At the very beginning of the church's life we read of Mr. and Mrs. Van Eddyngs, of the Orinoco River Mission of Venezuela, South America, addressing the congregation. Soon after this the church took upon itself the full support of two other missionaries at the same station, Miss Roe Williams, and the Rev. Arthur Tuggy. In June, 1925, an announcement read: "Mr. Vartan Atchinak, a converted Turk and a missionary to the Syrians in Palestine, will speak at Calvary Church Sunday evening. He will tell the thrilling story of his persecution at the hands of the Turks and tell how God miraculously delivered him time and again from Turkish persecution and court martial, while others were condemned to hang, and how God wonderfully preserved him at time of dire famine and pestilence." The same year another announcement reads: "The Calvary Church tabernacle was crowded Sunday evening to hear Mr. Young of Burma, India, give his splendid address. He told of the hundreds of conversions among the Burmas and Chinese." Some time later this statement was made to the church: "The friends of Calvary Church enjoyed the message brought by Miss Margarita Moran, missionary to the Telugu Indians of India, last Sunday morning. Miss Moran was formerly a society girl of New York City, but through the prayers of her mother, she was converted and immediately offered her services for work in India. She worked among these people many years and is about to return for the third time." Often Miss Martha Pohnert, a missionary from China, addressed the congregation. Soon after Mr. Fuller became pastor at Placentia, street meetings were begun when either Mr. Fuller or someone invited would preach the Gospel to these Orange Countians. In 1928 the Community Church at Olinda, previously known as the Olinda Methodist Church, asked the officers of Calvary Church to take over their work and the Sunday School there was conducted for some years, as long as there were workers residing there who were laboring in the nearby oil fields.

Calvary Church soon established a branch Sunday School at Santa Ana, which flourished, by the grace of God, so abundantly that by October, 1931, a church could be formed with an initial membership of one hundred and fifty. Often on Saturday a group of workers in the Calvary Church would go out into the highways of the northern part of Orange County and distribute circulars, announcing the services of the following Lord's Day. This is the way a church is built up and it will only be built up in this way when the pastor believes he has a message that people ought to hear. A Gospel team was organized, composed of young men from seven of the boys' clubs sponsored by the Church, which would go out for one meeting or a day's meetings, or for a week's services, and scores of people in Orange County were saved during the services these young men conducted. A Daily Vacation Bible School was soon organized. By 1928 the Calvary Church Sunday School was witnessing a regular attendance of over two hundred. We have thus far only been speaking about events, organizations, numbers, but of course back of all these things, in fact, the root and source of such growth is the personal life of the pastor and his people, the

GOD'S QUIET LEADING IN PLACENTIA

little things said and done, the prayers offered, the faithfulness of members, even those not too well known or with great gifts—just the unwearied, constant expenditure of time and strength and money in the Lord's work.

While Dr. Fuller, with his business burdens, his outside engagements, the necessity for constant study of the Word of God, and his own pulpit ministry at Calvary, never had leisure for engaging in the normal duties of a stated pastor, calling from home to home, yet there existed a deep love between the minister and his congregation. He was their leader; even the children knew this. When during one of the Anderson meetings, a boy was saved who was a regular attendant at the Sunday School and church, and the evangelist was calling forward those who had received Christ, the little fellow said, "If I go forward, I don't want to shake that man's hand. I want my own preacher to shake my hand." Many interesting anecdotes are told about the pastor. One of them is characteristic, it is said, of his entire ministry. A mother asked if he would dedicate her baby. His answer was, "I will have to search the Scriptures before I give you an answer." A week later he came back and said he would dedicate the child. He had found the answer in the story of Hannah and her boy, Samuel. While Dr. Fuller had seen to it, as the church building was designed and materials were settled upon, that the edifice should be in every way beautiful and commodious, he had made no provision for his own personal study. The notice in the newspaper of March 1, 1928, tells its own story: "While the Rev. Charles E. Fuller was absent at his labor for the Lord during the meetings which he held in Walla Walla, Washington, members of his congregation here were busy making plans for a pleasant surprise to be given him when he returned home. As a result of freewill contribution, members of the congregation furnished and decorated the study in Calvary Church where Mr. Fuller labors for so many hours each week in the preparation of the sermons that he uses in the Lord's work. While Mr. Fuller has seen to it that all the workers at the church have been well and comfortably equipped for their work, he has taken no thought for his own comfort. Four bare walls and the necessary books and desk were the furnishings of his study. Now a magnificent twelve by fifteen rug graces the floor, two oil paintings of California scenes adorn the walls, four potted ferns add their graceful beauty, and the study now presents a marked change for comfort as a result of the loving thoughts of Mr. Fuller's congregation."

One very important aspect of Mr. Fuller's ministry we have not mentioned, and that is the beginning of his radio ministry. This is so much of a subject of itself and leads directly into the great international broadcasts that were to develop after his leaving Calvary Church that we purposely have assigned this entire aspect of his Placentia work to another chapter.

The time now came for Mr. Fuller to feel that his work at Placentia was finished. All ministers who are active in the Lord's work and on the very front firing-line are bound to have some tribulation, almost always from those who could never do the kind of work that was being criticized. A few men here and there set about in a subtle way to woo away from the pastor the affections of his people. Upon one such individual subsequently the powerful hand of Divine judgment was laid, of which there is no need for a detailed discussion here. Mr. Fuller today, after seventeen years of absence from Placentia, has the same warm love of his congregation that he had when so faithfully laboring among them; they recognize that for those years they had in their midst one whom God called to one of the greatest ministries in the Gospel of the second quarter of the twentieth century. It was quite touching to see on Dr. Fuller's twenty-fourth anniversary of broadcasting a large group of people from Placentia, sitting together in a body in the great Civic Auditorium at Long Beach that Sunday afternoon. The son, Dan, of whom we shall speak elsewhere, preached so acceptably in his father's church a year ago that some in the congregation were overheard to say that some day he might be their pastor.

In the fall of 1921, Mr. Fuller enrolled as a student in the Bible Institute of Los Angeles, graduating in 1923, and returning for an additional year of work under Dr. Torrey. The Bible Institute of Los Angeles, now one of the greatest institutions of its kind in the western world, grew out of a Bible class organized in 1906 by the Rev. T. C. Horton, in the Immanuel Presbyterian Church, Los Angeles, soon to become famous among Christians everywhere by its name, "The Fisherman's Club." Mrs. Horton soon after opened a similar Bible class in a department store managed by Mr. D. H. Steel. A year later, with the co-operation of the Rev. A. B. Pritchard, pastor of the Central Presbyterian Church of the same city, some day classes were held in a building on South Main Street. In February, 1908, a permanent organization was effected, with the great Christian President of the Union Oil Co., Mr. Lyman Stewart as president, Mr. Pritchard as Vice-President, and Mr. Horton as superintendent. In 1911 the Board of Directors, believing that it was time for the school to enter upon a larger ministry, called Dr. Reuben Torrey as Dean. The invitation was accepted and Dr. Torrey served as Dean from January 1912 to 1924, as well as pastor of the great Church of the Open Door, which he organized in 1915.

When Charles Fuller entered as a student in the Bible Institute of Los Angeles, he was thirty-six years of age. At that time Dr. John MacInnis was the Professor of Christian Evidences and New Testament Exposition, and Dr. Alva J. McClain, for the last fifteen years the able president of Bethel Theological Seminary at Winona Lake, Indiana, was Professor of Bible Doctrine and Church History. John MacNeil, the famous Scotch evangelist, lectured on "The Preacher

With His Bible and Literature." But the outstanding teacher of those days was Dr. Torrey himself, who exercised an enormous influence over the thinking and public teaching and preaching of his student, Charles Fuller. A very sacred moment of those student days must here be referred to. Dr. Torrey taught a class in Teacher Training, in which Mr. Fuller was a pupil. One day it was the pupil's task to preach a sermon on Cain and Abel. When the message was finished and the pupil took his seat, Dr. Torrey sat for about two minutes looking straight ahead to the blackboard without a remark, and then so contrary to his usual way of speaking, as all who knew him will acknowledge, simply uttered this single sentence: "Young man, God has a great work ahead for you."

Strange how quickly a man grows, how rapidly things take place. Four years after graduation Dr. Fuller was made Secretary of the Board of Directors. In 1929 he was made Chairman of the Board and continued to serve as such down to 1932, five years of hard work, many meetings, heartaches, financial problems, administrative burdens, all done that the Word of God might be taught to these young men and women and missionaries and ministers sent out to hold forth the Word of Life. At this time Dr. William P. White, gracious teacher of the Word, was President of Biola, and Mr. William A. Fisher, Executive Vice-President. Mrs. Lyman Stewart served at this time as Secretary, who with the others named, and Mr. Leon B. Shaw, made up the Executive Committee. The other members of the Board of Directors in the year, 1929, were Mr. Joseph W. Cline, the Rev. W. E. Edmonds, Mr. Howard Frost, Mr. Adolph Larson, Mr. Nathan Newby, and Mr. J. O. Smith. In 1930 Dr. Charles G. Trumbull also served as a member of the Board of Directors.

Through all these years, the Lord was preparing his servant, Charles Fuller, for a mightier ministry than he could have at this time imagined. His qualifications for this work, without which the great tasks which God would soon put upon his shoulders could not be fulfilled, were being developed. At the time of his conversion, the Spirit of God had created two deep, life-long passions in his heart—a love for the Word of God, and a love for the souls of men. His knowledge of the Word had now been broadened and deepened; his love for souls was manifested in his constant ministry of evangelism. God had given him a gift for making the truth of His Word clear and plain to the common people, and to others too, as often happens. Mr. Fuller had a good, sound knowledge of music, and was able to sing, talents which, of course, he had long before conversion. He had now learned something of the work, the trials, the joys, of an active pastor. God had raised up a host of friends for him, some of them among the outstanding Christian leaders of our country. He had known the abundant blessing of God upon his labors, nothing phenomenal, nothing that drew national attention, not vast crowds following him across the country, but still the constant, consistent harvesting of souls as the result of his faithful preaching of the Word of God. In addition to all these, trials had multiplied, testings had come upon him from many directions, and he had learned what it was to rest in the Lord in dark hours when man had failed. In other words, he was growing up in Christ Jesus, into a greater fullness of manhood. His ear was open to the whisperings of the Holy Spirit. He knew what it was to get answers in prayer. Now all of these things have often been true of faithful disciples without anything unusual taking place in subsequent days, but God had determined in His holy council to separate unto Himself for an international ministry this orange grower and student of the Word. How God revealed this, and something of the great ways in which God phenomenally blessed his work will occupy us in the next two chapters.

Chapter VIII

"BROUGHT VERY LOW"

Eliphaz, in his first discourse with Job, at the time of his great afflictions, uttered a sentence which is not only world famous, but undeniably true—"Man is born unto trouble, as the sparks fly upward" (Job 5:7). Trouble comes not only to men who live without God, but to men who walk with God. Abraham, father of the faithful, found his herdsmen quarrelling with those of Lot, and must needs propose a plan which would bring about a state of at least temporary peace; years later he had his heart torn by a command from God to take his only son Isaac to the top of Mount Moriah, where he had expected to offer him as a sacrifice. Joseph, one of the purest characters that ever lived, suffered from the jealousies of his own family, was nigh unto death as his brothers cast him into a cistern, was thrown into prison, unjustifiably accused by Potiphar's wife. Moses must flee from Egypt forty years, and then for forty more, great lawgiver and prophet that he was, must endure the constant murmurings of the great Israelitish host. David knew troubles from every direction, was pursued relentlessly from cave to cave by Saul whom he had served, and later was compelled to forsake his throne and flee from Jerusalem in the rebellion of his own son Absalom. It was at the time of Saul's pursuit of him that David uttered the 142d Psalm, which might well begin our brief chapter:

"I cried unto the Lord with my voice; with my voice unto the Lord did I make supplication. I poured out my complaint before him; I shewed before him my trouble. When my spirit was overwhelmed within me, then thou knewest my path. In the way where I walked have they privily laid a snare for me. I looked on my right hand, and beheld, but there was no man that would know me: refuge failed me; no man cared for my soul. I cried unto thee, O Lord: I said, Thou art my refuge and my portion in the land of the living. Attend unto my cry; for I am brought very low; deliver me from my persecutors; for they are stronger than I. Bring my soul out of prison, that I may praise thy name: the righteous shall compass me about; for thou shalt deal bountifully with me."

Trouble, anxiety, heavy burdens, disappointments, heartaches, have been the experience of Charles E. Fuller, not only in the days before he gave his heart to Christ, but often with even greater force and weight in the years when he was faithfully serving the Lord. The year after his marriage, five years before he was saved, when managing his own orange grove, and living in his recently purchased home, a terrible freeze hit Southern California, destroying almost all of his fruit. In 1913, an even more severe freeze not only ruined the orange crop, but in many cases utterly wiped out whole orange groves; water would get into the bark and split it, the tender roots were often frozen as the unusual weather penetrated the normally warm ground. For mile after mile one could see defoliated orange groves with the ruined fruit hanging on the bare branches. Though Charles had amply provided his grove with orchard heaters, that freeze in January, 1913, was one the heaters could not counteract. Long before midnight, hundreds of citrus growers knew that it was useless any longer to feed oil to these belching stoves, and aware that he had lost everything except his wife and her love, Mr. Fuller retired for such sleep as such a night would afford. The grove had to be abandoned, and in a mood of depression, the Fullers decided to leave Redlands.

Hearing that a packing house in the town of Placentia was looking for a manager, Charles Fuller, now thirty years of age, in the very prime and vigor of life, applied for a position, and obtained it, with the Mutual Packing Association, which offered him, after a prolonged conference, a three months' trial at a salary of one hundred dollars a month! To Placentia they then moved, away from lovely Redlands and all the memories of school and home, fifty miles distant. Here they first lived in a small rented house, but shortly after were able to purchase a home of four rooms next door to the Women's Club, located on the corner of Bradford and Chapman Avenues.

In 1929 came the great crash. Mr. Fuller had 250 acres of orange groves on his hands, which in normal times could have been completely paid for within a few years, but with the market gone, the banks closing, and credit tightening, like thousands of other business men, careful as they had been in every transaction, Mr. Fuller found himself in an ever-tightening vise, with creditors pressing him on every side. Long meetings with those involved, in Los Angeles, day after day, extended into months, as the young Christian fought to keep off bankruptcy, believing that obligations should be met and not avoided. The printed page cannot communicate the exhausting experiences through which Mr. Fuller went in those days, and the terrible toll it took upon his strength.

Another burden was now to be added. There had come to bless the Fuller home on August 28, 1925, a precious baby boy, named Daniel Payton, soon to develop into a robust, healthy child. When four-and-a-half years of age, just in the most trying days of the depression, he developed pneumonia from a case of whooping cough, and the following year, the father still fighting to keep some of his property, Dan was afflicted again with pneumonia, this time of a most virulent type. He gradually grew worse until his flesh had wasted away, and at times he lay in his little bed unconscious. When the crisis came, the turn was for the worse, and the little one was seen to be choking for breath. A pulmotor was brought in, which temporarily gave the needed relief. Mr. Fuller was engaged at the time in one of his many long conferences concerning business matters in Los Angeles. Called on the phone, he left immediately for his home, fearful that this would be the day in which his little son would be taken from them. Weary with financial problems, exhausted from heavy duties at the church, his whole being, body, mind, and soul, near a breaking point, like John the Baptist in the prison near the Dead Sea, he began to question everything and as he drove wildly out of the city, he told the Lord that if his little boy should be taken, he would be *through*—no more Christian service for him, no more trying to preach the gospel. But as mile after mile was covered, the Spirit of God worked a miracle of change in his heart, and by the time he reached his home, he told the Lord that if it was His will to take the child, he would still trust Him, and be His servant to the uttermost. As he went in and knelt down by the bed of his unconscious son, now blue in face, Charles Fuller weepingly uttered a prayer to God which Mrs. Fuller can still recall: "I thank you, Lord, for these five-and-a-half years that we have had this little boy. He has been such a blessing in our home. We shall miss him so, but take him to Yourself if that is Your will. 'The Lord has given, and the Lord has taken away, blessed be the name of the Lord.' We are giving him back to you, our Father." The ambulance was at the door, and the lad was rushed to a Los Angeles hospital, but a change had come, no doubt in answer to prayer. The fluoroscope showed no indication that any particles were stopping the normal functions of the lung; something had been absorbed so that breathing now began to resume normally. The tokens of pneumonia were still there, but there was hope for his recovery. God graciously brought him through this deep valley, but six years were to go by before he had fully recovered from the illness that had so depleted his strength and emaciated his little body. From that time on he grew rapidly, and today Dan is an upstanding, strong young man, six feet high, two hundred pounds of solid manhood.

There was only one more major area in Mr. Fuller's life in which troubles *could* arise, and that would be the church, and there they did arise. Financially driven to the wall, Mrs. Fuller still weak from a major operation, little Dan only slowly creeping back to health, friends now mysteriously began to forsake him. Unjustified criticism arose, fault-finding became prevalent, and sometimes even evil things were said about this hard-pressed servant of God. Oh, how many there are who have given everything to their Lord, have served Him day and night, only to come to an hour when they find those who do little for Christ uttering malicious falsehoods born of an evil heart and spread by lips that are not under the control of the Spirit of God. This was the time when the Word of God became precious, when, like Jeremiah of old, Mr. Fuller day after day would have to spread out before the Lord the things that others were saying, and all the rest of his troubles. They were bewildering days, days of testing, but a promise of an older day, made through the great prophet Isaiah was now being fulfilled: "When thou passest through the waters, I will be with thee; and through the rivers, they shall not overflow thee: when thou walkest through the fire, thou shalt not be burned; neither shall the flame kindle upon thee" (Isa. 43:2). Like David of old, and many of the children of God of every generation since, Dr. Fuller knew the meaning of the words of the Psalmist: "I cried unto God with my voice, even unto God with my voice; and he gave ear unto me. In the day of my trouble I sought the Lord: my sore ran in the night, and ceased not: my soul refused to be comforted. I remembered God, and was troubled: I complained and my spirit was overwhelmed. Thou holdest mine eyes waking: I am so troubled that I cannot speak" (Ps. 77: 1-4).

The Apostle Peter, in speaking of the heaviness that comes to many children of God through manifold testings, declares these experiences are sent to us of God, "That the trial of your faith, being much more precious than of gold that perisheth, though it be tried with fire, might be found unto praise and honour and glory at the appearing of Jesus Christ" (I Peter 1:7). The testing by fire certainly was there. Mr. Fuller at one time was fifty pounds below his normal weight, through fatigue and discouragement. However, he did not go to pieces, he did not rebel against the Lord, he did not go to court, he did not stir up a church fight. He put these things in the hands of the Lord. He felt the time had come to resign his pastorate at Placentia, and at the same time was finally forced to give up all of his orange grove property in the Placentia area. This was followed by the moving of the Fuller family to San Marino, on the outskirts of lovely Pasadena. The gold was now free of much dross, scorching as were the flames that removed it, and, though he did not know it, Mr. Fuller now stood on the threshold of a ministry greater than any he would ever have had even if pastor of the largest Protestant church of California; for he was soon to be heralding the message of the grace of God into homes that had never heard the gospel, and to millions of living souls every Lord's Day afternoon. The words of the hymn that we often sing so glibly had now been indelibly written into the heart of this stalwart disciple of Christ:

> "When thro' fiery trials thy pathway shall lie,
> My grace all sufficient shall be thy supply;
> The flame shall not hurt thee; I only design
> Thy dross to consume, and thy gold to refine."

The words the apostle Paul once used in writing of himself, were soon to be true in the ministry of Charles E. Fuller—"as poor, yet making many rich."

Chapter IX

GIRDLING THE GLOBE WITH THE GOSPEL

The Christian religion is an oral religion. It was announced by prophets, it was ushered into the world with the songs of angels. Jesus is announced at the theshold of His ministry with the words "Jesus came preaching." He was called The Teacher Come from God and of Him all who heard were compelled to say "never man spake as this man." Of His own words, all of them orally delivered, none of them written by Himself in a book, He said: "Heaven and earth shall pass away but my words shall never pass away." When the Lord was about to ascend, His commission to the disciples was that they were to go everywhere preaching. The book of Acts is a story of the oral utterances of the apostles and evangelists of the early church and the consequences that flowed from their powerful deliverances. All down through the ages has Christianity propagated itself by oral utterances—the preaching of the Gospel—and established itself by teaching, by schools in which the Truth was unfolded. Of all the various ministries of the Christian Church, more than any other, evangelism is an oral phenomenon.

The subject of our biography, by a revolutionary invention discovered and developed all within his life time, has been able in four half-hour messages to reach more living people on this earth than the greatest evangelist of the nineteenth century, D. L. Moody, was able to reach, with long journeys, fatiguing travels, and sometimes three meetings a day, in his entire forty years of Christian service. How this

GIRDLING THE GLOBE WITH THE GOSPEL 111

came about is something we ought now to carefully consider, for the story behind broadcasting is one of the most wonderful tales in human history.

Centuries ago in the days when speech was so seriously considered an art, when the foundations of philosophy for all time were being laid, Socrates said to Gorgias: "What is that which you say is the greatest good of man and of which you are the creator; answer us." Gorgias replied: "That good, Socrates, which is truly the greatest, being that which gives to men freedom in their own persons and to individuals with power of ruling over others in their several states." "And what would you consider this to be?" asked Socrates, to which Gorgias replied: "What is there greater than the word which persuades the judges in the courts or the senators in the council or the citizens in the assembly or in any other political meeting? If you have the power of uttering this word, you will have the physician your slave and the trainer your slave and the money maker of whom you talk will be found to gather treasures, not for himself but for you who are able to speak and persuade the multitude." The broadcasting of the Gospel in which Mr. Fuller has been engaged now this quarter of a century has really proved to be that agency, far beyond anything that these Greek philosophers ever dreamed of, "which gives to men freedom in their own persons," and this freedom given to them through Jesus Christ and not in relation to money changers and political powers, but freely—by grace.

It is one of those strange coincidences of history that the very year in which Charles E. Fuller was born was also the year in which, across the waters, in Germany, a scientist made a discovery which became the cornerstone of all broadcasting in the world, the year 1887. For this we must go even further back for a moment. Faraday, the famous English physicist, in 1831 discovered what is called electromagnetic induction, a phrase which means simply this—that when a great deal of electricity is turned on and off in a wire, it is capable of producing a similar intermittent current in another circuit not directly connected with it. That means that a current of electricity flowing through a coil of wire in one corner of a room is able to reproduce a current in another coil of wire with which it is not attached, in the opposite corner of the room. Faraday did not live to see the ultimate, vast consequences of this fundamental discovery. In fact, he did not know the exact nature of this phenomenon. Truth is, we do not wholly understand it yet, though we know its laws.

In 1887, a brilliant pupil of Helmholtz, Heinrich Rudolf Hertz, afterward professor of physics in the technical high school at Karlsruhe, later a professor at Bonn— after a year's experimenting in his laboratory, goaded on by the brilliant mathematical conclusions of Clerk Maxwell, demonstrated the possibility of creating electromagnetic waves in the ether. He succeeded not only in discovering these waves but in accurately measuring their velocity and length, and finally demonstrated that these electromagnetic waves were of the same speed as light waves. This suggested that light might be a form of electromagnetic energy, and it was finally realized that light waves and radiant heat waves were also electromagnetic, consisting of two parts—an electric wave and a magnetic wave—each perpendicular to the other and both at right angles to their direction. Hertz died at the early age of thirty-two, in 1894, but just at this time a brilliant Italian by the name of Marconi, realizing the significance of what are now called Hertzian waves, conceived the idea of putting messages on these waves. He was successful, in short distances, as early as 1892, when twenty-eight years old. In June, 1896, he filed an application for a patent on an invention of which the patent read: "Electrical actions or manifestations are transmitted through the air, earth, or water by means of elec-

GIRDLING THE GLOBE WITH THE GOSPEL 113

tric oscillation of high frequency." Marconi's life is a series of wonders—everything short of a miracle! He was brilliant, persistent, and consistently successful.

By 1899, in spite of much public ridicule, the International Yacht Race was reported by wireless. In 1901, messages were electrically transmitted across the Atlantic Ocean without wire or cable. By February, 1902, messages could be sent by wireless at as great a distance as 3,000 miles. This was revolutionary, and Marconi, with others, realized that it would soon be possible to girdle the globe with electric communication through the air.

We must now come down to the winter of 1919 and visit the city of Pittsburgh. Dr. Frank Conrad, an engineer of the Westinghouse Electric Manufacturing Company, of East Pittsburgh, was working on a special radio telephone transmitter for the Navy. He had rigged up a considerable laboratory in his own home. By this time there were of course a number of amateurs setting up instruments and receiving aerial messages. He hit upon the idea of playing phonograph records in his laboratory, and soon fifteen or twenty amateurs were regularly listening to these embryonic concerts. By the summer of 1920 these programs had become so popular that a Pittsburgh department store advertised for sale: "Approved radio receiving sets for listening to Dr. Conrad's concerts."

It was at this point that radio really took hold of the American public, and grew with greater strides into a vast industry and into a factor of enormous influence in human life, than any other single invention of all times with the exception of the gasoline engine. Under the auspices of the Westinghouse Electric and Manufacturing Company, station KDKA was formally opened on Election Night, November 2, 1920. By December 1922, there were 508 stations broadcasting programs and by 1923 there were more than 1,000 radio broadcasting stations in North America! The Radio Corporation of America had been formed at a capitalization of forty million dollars. By 1926 the sales of radio apparatus in the United States alone amounted to over $400,000,000! Within twenty years after Dr. Frank Conrad's first concert, radio broadcasting had become such a powerful, widely established factor in the life of the citizens of the United States that President Franklin D. Roosevelt in one broadcast in September spoke to at least ninety million people at one time.

And what is broadcasting? I think we might here take the definition of a standard work on broadcasting published twenty years ago. "Broadcasting is a question of picking up sounds, translating those sounds into the electrical language, thundering that language to any desired degree of intensity by the process known as amplification, loading up a radio vehicle (properly called the carrier wave) with the desired sounds by means of modulation, transporting the sounds far and wide and unloading an infinitesimal part of the carrier waves' secret at the doorsteps of every home." The same writers inform us that if a man added the power of one human voice to his voice power every second for every hour, day and night of every day in the year, it would take him and his descendants 1,600 years to pile up a voice as strong as that of a voice going out over a standard broadcasting station.

"Broadcasting," says Professor Robinson in a recent book published by Columbia University, "has become the most effective means for mass communication in the history of the world."

Probably there are six major spheres of what might be called broadcasting material. There is advertising stuff; there are the programs for education, including musical programs; there are programs primarily produced for entertainment; there are news programs; and finally, there are what might be called propoganda programs which may originate from a

GIRDLING THE GLOBE WITH THE GOSPEL 115

political party or from a national government. And then there are religious programs, and in this area we are of course interested in this chapter. It has been estimated that about five per cent of all radio programmes are to be classified as religious.

Religious broadcasting is generally acknowledged to have begun, in this country, January 2, 1921, when a service was broadcast from the Calvary Episcopal Church of East Liberty, Pittsburgh by its pastor, Dr. E. J. Van Etten. Six years later, Mr. H. P. Davis, vice-president of the Western Electric and Manufacturing Company, in an address given at the great School of Business Administration at Harvard, said of Dr. Van Etten: "His was the first voice to be heard in a broadcasting of divine services and through his enthusiasm in this work he has undoubtedly done more to bring happiness and religious comfort to the masses of people than any other living man." It was not long before three men whom we might call early giants of religious broadcasting arose, strange to say, two of them (the latter two of the three here to be mentioned) outstanding liberals. The National Broadcasting Company used regularly three religious programs on the Lord's Day, one conducted by Dr. Poling, President of the Greater New York Federation of Churches at that time, the program being called the National Youth Radio Conference. Then Dr. S. Parks Cadman with his crowded men's service on Sunday afternoon at the Bedford Branch of the Y.M.C.A. in Brooklyn, and Dr. Harry Emerson Fosdick, radically liberal minister of the Riverside Church, New York, possessing brilliant preaching gifts and a marvellously persuasive voice and transparent language, drew millions to their radio every Sunday afternoon to listen to their messages, so devoid of any Gospel of the redeeming work of the Son of God. Strange to say, none of these programs has been on the air for years. Dr. Poling's program probably had the shortest life. Dr. S. Parks Cadman's work ended with his death in 1935. Dr. Fosdick's program somehow shrivelled up in the last few years of his ministry, and his grip upon the American public was greatly slackened. Though he is still living, he is not, as a rule, broadcasting.

One outstanding conservative, however, was able to finance a national Bible teaching and Gospel preaching program, conducting it with unusual brilliance—my friend, Dr. Donald Grey Barnhouse. For some years this program had been allowed to lapse, but we are glad to say has now been vigorously revived.

We must now turn to the subject of this biography, who, by the leading of God, was to become one of the outstanding figures in religious broadcasting in America, during the second quarter of our century. We should go back for a moment to a line of development in his boyhood days that was purposely eliminated when we were watching him at Redlands and Pomona. During the years 1905 and 1906, Mr. Fuller, then just finishing high school, became deeply interested in telephonic and telegraphic communication. He had a friend, Jim Rimpau, who was employed by the Santa Fe Railroad at Redlands Junction, from whom he learned the Morse Code; in fact, often while Jim was out sealing cars, young Fuller was recording messages coming over the telegraph ticker in the railroad station, and in cases of urgency, was sending out messages. The other station-masters along the line were able to distinguish between Jim's telegraphing and that of Charles, but they liked the young lad and never reported that he was often functioning as a self-appointed telegrapher of the rapidly growing Southwest. As soon as wireless equipment was available, Charles bought a set. His father thought the thing was more or less of a fraud. One afternoon a wireless message was sent out from Catalina that a Congressman, engaged in deep-sea fishing near-by had caught a

260-pound fish. Charles ran in to tell his father what he had just heard. The father's reaction, expressed with fervent scorn was summed up in one word, "Fiddlesticks." However, the next morning the same item appeared in the Los Angeles *Times,* which Charles was not slow to show to his father, whose only reply was, "I'll be jiggered." God was even then getting this young man ready for radio work, so that, different from a great many preachers who have used the wonderful facilities of radio communication, Charles Fuller knew something of the technicalities and the science of the wonderful modern invention with which he has been identified for so many years.

The first broadcasting work that Mr. Fuller did was in 1924, in the month of October, when twice a week he spoke for the Bible Institute of Los Angeles over its station, KTBI. The class was called, using these letters, "Knowledge Through Bible Instruction." No records were kept of this so-called radio school of the Bible, and just what Mr. Fuller said at that time it is not possible to recall.

In 1927, Mr. Fuller, attending a Bible conference in Indianapolis, was, without warning, asked to substitute for the regular speaker on a gospel radio program. Apparently the radio was built for Charles Fuller, or Charles Fuller was built for radio preaching, for the following day he was told that an unusual number of letters had been received telling of blessing that had come through hearing his message of the day before on Mark 4:35–41. This probably served to stir up his heart, and to make him think, hope, dream, and even pray for an extended ministry through this new and marvelous medium. The same week he was in a Pullman berth on his way west. On traveling from Philadelphia to Chicago, and asleep, he was suddenly awakened, conscious of a divine urgency, and had revealed to him not only the enormous possibilities of a radio ministry, but that God wanted *him* to undertake this. His normal shyness now manifested itself, and like Moses of old, when God told him he was to go before Pharaoh and ask for the release of the enslaved children of Israel, Mr. Fuller entered into a long argument with the Spirit of God about the whole program suddenly displayed before him. It was not a quiet episode, rather, a convulsive one. He turned over in the berth, rose up in a position of kneeling and for three hours he wrestled with God, and God wrestled with him, regarding what was to be, though he did not know it at the time, his great life work. Finally he told the Lord that if He would go with him, he would accept this challenge, and would with His help, undertake definite broadcasting.

Plans were at once entered upon, and in February, 1928, broadcasts began from Calvary Church at Placentia, both at the morning and evening services of the Lord's Day. Later he added a Thursday evening Bible class. An early announcement in the local newspaper reads as follows: "Everything is in readiness at Calvary church for the first broadcasting of the Sunday evening services by remote control over radio station KREG, Santa Ana, on February 23 at 8 o'clock. The local church is the first in Orange County to establish a regular broadcasting feature, as arrangements have been made to be on the air each Sunday from eight to nine o'clock. Station KREG will be found at 1500 kilocycles, three points below KECA on the radio dial. For the service dedicating the new broadcast feature, Rev. Charles E. Fuller will preach from the subject, "The Greatest Peril of the Hour." From KREG the broadcast was soon shifted to KGER, the 1000 watt Long Beach station. Even then Mr. Leland Green was the announcer in full charge of the radio programs. He is still in charge of this part of the work for Dr. Fuller, and is a master in this intricate art. To the millions of people who have often wondered how, week after week, the whole hour of broadcasting could flow with such perfect smoothness, without hesitation or an embarrassing interruption, it must be said that a great deal of this is due to the meticulous way in which Mr. Green first plots out the entire program, then supervises the rehearsal, and, finally, guides the actual broadcast.

In the year before Mr. Fuller left Placentia, an event took place which, at the time, was probably considered as an episode of no particular, far-reaching importance, but which became a large and vital factor in all the years that followed in the great world-wide programs that were soon to be launched. There came into Mr. Fuller's study one day a very quiet-mannered man, originating from Butte, Montana, by the name of R. H. Alber, thirty-six years of age, who was just beginning to build up an advertising company specializing in radio work. He asked Mr. Fuller if he could not become his radio agent, and Mr. Fuller, impressed with his quiet ways, and knowing that someone soon would have to manage this part of the work, turned over this increasingly important business to the visitor. Mr. Alber was with him until the day of his death, in January of this year. He never missed a broadcast, and often traveled with Mr. Fuller across the country attending his great mass meetings. Absolutely trustworthy, as Mr. Fuller's broadcast grew, he grew with it, until the time came when the R. H. Alber Company of Los Angeles would be one of the outstanding radio agents in America.

After leaving the pastorate of Calvary Church, Mr. Fuller felt that God was clearly leading him to devote all of his time to the proclamation of the gospel and teaching the Word of God over the radio, and a contract was entered into for a Sunday morning and Sunday evening service, each one hour in length, to be released from the studio of KGER, Long Beach. Little did those entering into this contract know that within a few weeks, on March 10, 1933, California would be shaken with a violent earthquake. Three days later, a moratorium was declared, and all banks were temporarily closed. Without resources of his own, Mr. Fuller was wholly dependent upon the gifts of God's children for this work. The morning service from 11–12 o'clock each Sunday was called the Pilgrim Hour, in which, in addition to beautiful music, there was a systematic interpretation of the Word of God, a service of an expository nature; the evening hour was devoted to the preaching of the gospel. In the spring of 1935, Mr. Fuller had just sixty names on his mailing list, men and women who, having faith in him, and believing in the need for such broadcast services, were holding him up in prayer and encouraging him by the financial support of his work. It was at this time that the famous Heart-to-Heart Talks originated, a series that has been maintained regularly every month for fifteen consecutive years. It was also about this time that Mr. Fuller took on a contract with two 50,000-watt stations, KFI in Los Angeles, and KNX in Hollywood, in addition to carrying three regular weekly programs over KGER in Long Beach. The original KNX program was for thirty minutes, but in 1935 he felt led to extend it to an hour, knowing that this powerful station reached as far north as Alaska and deep into Mexico, and often crossed the Rocky Mountains. He thought he might encourage an audience for these broadcasts, and at a cost of $350.00 a week—a huge sum in those days for this type of work—he engaged the auditorium of the Hollywood Women's Club. Ridicule followed, even on the part of many of his friends. On the first evening, Mrs. Fuller, who had not generally attended the broadcasts at the various studios, accompanied her beloved husband to the first service at the Hollywood Women's Club. Fifty persons were present, in a room that seats four hundred! A dozen volunteers carried the musical program of the service, and here, in this most insignificant way, began the Old Fashioned Revival Hour, in the city of the movies, but

Dr. Fuller at the Microphone

GIRDLING THE GLOBE WITH THE GOSPEL 121

also the city where Charles Fuller gave his heart to God, and where this mighty force for Christ may be said to have been born.

Two years later, Dr. Fuller became attached, for the first time, to a great network. A word probably should be said about networks in this place, for many who daily listen to programs for which networks are responsible know very little about the machinery and setup for such a complicated organization; and inasmuch as it was a network that carried Dr. Fuller's message around the world, perhaps we would more clearly understand what was soon to take place if we have before us some information concerning this particular aspect of broadcasting. Let me quote, then, the first five paragraphs from an official communication recently distributed by one of the large broadcasting company services of this country:

"A radio 'network,' as the term is used in the broadcasting industry, is a company which engages in the business of supplying programs to a group of 'affiliated stations,' the programs being fed to the various stations by telephone lines from the network's studios, so that they are broadcast by a hundred or more stations simultaneously. Almost half of all the programs heard by radio listeners over American radio stations are programs produced by networks; nearly 70 per cent of all commercial radio stations are affiliated with networks and receive network programs for broadcasting, and the daily program schedule of the average network affiliated station will include from four or five hours to as much as 10 to 12 hours of network programs.

"Nearly forty different networks provide American radio stations with programs today. All but four of these are regional in scope, with affiliated stations limited to a single state or to three or four adjoining states. At the beginning of 1944, 220 different radio stations out of the total of more than 900 commercial stations in the United States were affiliated with regional networks. However, all but 10 of these stations were also affiliated with one or more of the national networks; and the total sale of time by regional networks amounted to only a little more than one per cent of the dollar volume of network time sales in the United States. The four national networks are the National Broadcasting Company, organized in 1926; the Columbia Broadcasting System, which came into being the following year; the Mutual Broadcasting System, which began operations in 1935; and the Blue Network, originally a part of the National Broadcasting Company but separated from NBC and set up as an independent corporation in February, 1942.

"Each national network maintains studios for the production of network programs in each of four or five key cities— usually New York, Washington, Chicago, and Hollywood. In these key cities, programs are originated in studios owned by the network directly, or in those of 'key stations,' owned by or affiliated with the network. From the network originating point, programs are piped by telephone lines to the control boards in the studios of the various affiliated stations throughout the country. In most cases, the same program is fed to all of the network's affiliated stations; at times, however, two or more programs may originate simultaneously in different key cities, each being fed to a 'split network' including stations in one particular section of the country. Differences in time between the eastern and central states and those on the Pacific Coast, for instance, make it desirable to provide repeat broadcasts of many programs at a later time for stations on the West Coast; at such time, other programs are usually made available by the network to affiliated stations in the eastern and central states.

"At the beginning of 1944, Mutual had 212 affiliates; Columbia had 136; the National Broadcasting Company had 136; and the Blue Network had 176 affiliated stations. Of the

GIRDLING THE GLOBE WITH THE GOSPEL

total 46 stations were at the same time affiliated with two of the four national networks, so that 625 of the 908 commercial stations then licensed by the government had national network affiliations." Of the American Broadcasting Company we will speak later.

In January, 1937, the Old Fashioned Revival Hour began flowing over the Mutual network, which at that time consisted of thirteen stations, and bringing the message as far east as Gary, Indiana, just a little south of Chicago. But hardly six months had passed when something happened which could have meant a violent and tragic end to the entire program. In August, Mr. Alber brought to Mr. Fuller's office the inside information that an eastern corporation with great wealth was on the verge of entering into a contract with the Mutual network for a coast-to-coast hook-up, which would embrace all the stations then using the Old Fashioned Revival Hour release. After a moment's meditation, rising to his feet and looking into his friend's face, Mr. Fuller quietly replied, "Rudy, tell the Mutual Broadcasting System that the Old Fashioned Revival Hour will take the network coast-to-coast."

"Can you make it, Charlie?" said the agent, who knew all the obligations that such a contract would involve, and who also was intimately acquainted with the resources at Mr. Fuller's disposal.

"No," said Mr. Fuller, "I cannot, but God can."

It was only five years since Mr. Fuller had resigned from the pastorate of a church of less than five hundred members, and he was now to speak to millions. This being of the Lord, it meant Charles E. Fuller was ready to speak to a world-wide audience. Growth, deep spiritual growth must have been the experience of those years—by study, prayer, victory, patience, obedience. Some remain babes in Christ, some grow to mature manhood; a few attain gigantic stature.

In five weeks the change was made, and from 13 stations

the Old Fashioned Revival Hour moved into 65 stations, with the weekly expenditure raised from $1441 to $4500. By October of the following year, the number of stations had reached 117; by 1940, 150 stations were carrying it, and in 1943—a tremendous figure and nothing less than a miracle—the Old Fashioned Revival Hour was going out over 1000 stations, reaching a potential audience of over two million people, with expenses rising as high as $40,000 a week! The public should know that there are no charge accounts in radio broadcasting; in fact, you do not pay for what you *have* used, you have a check in the office of the corporation on Friday for what you *intend* to use on Sunday. In September of 1942, the full sixty minutes of the Pilgrim Hour was added. In December of that year, the Old Fashioned Revival Hour was rebroadcast over the Pacific area, on the Don Lee Broadcasting System, a part of Mutual, from 10:00–11:00 every Sunday night, for the benefit of those who were compelled to work in the war plants all day. This schedule continued to May of 1944, when the Pilgrim Hour was dropped from the Mutual network. In September of that year, the Mutual Broadcasting System's policy of no religious programs after twelve o'clock noon, Eastern Standard Time, and only one-half hour in duration, became effective, and the Old Fashioned Revival Hour was dropped. The Pilgrim Hour was reduced to thirty minutes and released on Mutual during morning hours. Because it was able to secure the interest of independent stations, the Old Fashioned Revival Hour continued.

Just before his death, Mr. Alber placed in my hands a statistical summary of his work with Mr. Fuller in the Old Fashioned Revival Hour alone, and it seems to me this information is so important that it ought to be placed here in this volume, statistical as it is:

Total Pressings—250,000
Total number of Acetates—15,000

GIRDLING THE GLOBE WITH THE GOSPEL

Total number of metal parts—20,000
Total pounds of copper—38,000
Total pounds of Vinylite—250,000
Total pounds of silver used in preparation of electro plates —475
Total number of labels—1,000,000
Feet of acetate thread cut from acetates—15,000,000
Total number of words spoken (on basis of 125 words per minute)—2,437,500
Accumulated number of hours broadcast—24 hours a day for 482 days
Accumulated number of minutes broadcast—694,080
If each transcription was set edge to edge the number of transcriptions made would measure 4½ miles.
Total number of people involved each week in making and releasing the program over 500 radio stations in the United States and other countries—3,500.

What this coast-to-coast and later around-the-world broadcast, week after week, sometimes repeated three times on a Sunday, and then, by recordings, rebroadcast from any number of stations that chose to use the message, has meant to literally millions of people can only be partially known, and only fragmentarily recorded. It meant, to begin with, that hundreds of thousands of people who could not get to church would be hearing the gospel preached, clearly, lovingly, and with power—the mountaineers of Kentucky, the cowboys in their ranch houses, families weary with the week's work in homes fifty miles from the nearest church, women in kitchens, lighthouse keepers, forest rangers, now could hear the gospel and the most beautiful religious music that has probably ever floated across the ether waves of our land in regular everyweek programmes. Invalids at home, the sick and dying in hospitals, prisoners locked in their cells, those with mental afflictions confined to state and county institutions, the aged in old people's homes, could all have one hour of heaven upon earth. In thousands of saloons throughout the land would the gospel music be turned on, even men in their cups would not want to miss what they knew was from the Lord indeed, from whom they were trying to flee; automobiles crowding the lanes and highways of our land could tune in to this uplifting hour. Even people reclining on the beaches, or in the mountain summer resorts, with small hand radios could let their souls bathe in this hour of spiritual lift. Hundreds of congregations without pastors, unable to secure the services of a local preacher, could gather together in a place of worship, or at a home, and listen to one of the rarest hours of divine service that God has allowed any man to create in our generation. When a heavy blanket of snow confined millions of farmers to their homes, or rainstorms made roads impassable, the Lord's Day need not pass without such music as few church choirs can produce, and a message around which hours of prayer had gathered.

And then came the war! O, how God did know what He was doing when He brought the Old Fashioned Revival Hour into existence at such an early date, so that by the time war did break out, the whole earth could listen to this message: the thousands and hundreds of thousands of marines, sailors, soldiers, members of the air force, wounded servicemen in hospitals, great multitudes massed together in camps, some sick with tropical fevers, others on the high seas not knowing when the moment might arrive when a bomb would shatter their ship and they would be thrown into the sea, nurses weary with their exhausting duties, men and women everywhere nauseated with the horrors, the vice, and the brutality of war—all were bound together in one great world-wide family as they listened, one hour, some early in the morning, some at noon, some in the afternoon, some in early evening, others far into the night, to a message of grace and love, of

GIRDLING THE GLOBE WITH THE GOSPEL 127

forgiveness and cleansing, of redemption and hope, from God through the lips of His consecrated servant. What an opportunity that was, and how it was seized to the uttermost. Thousands of men and women went to their death saved by Christ through the Old Fashioned Revival Hour. Thousands living today can bear a similar testimony. Sometimes in meetings Dr. Fuller has asked for hands of those who were saved while listening to the Old Fashioned Revival Hour, and, in some large assemblies, over a thousand hands would be raised at one service.

Some years ago the most gifted conservative religious journalist of our country at that time, Dr. Charles E. Trumbull, a close friend, a frequent visitor, and staunch supporter of Dr. Fuller wrote, as he could in his inimitable style, for the paper he was so brilliantly editing, the *Sunday School Times* of Philadelphia, an account of one of the Old Fashioned Revival Services, and I think, though it has been frequently reprinted, it belongs here in this chapter:

"On a Sunday evening in August, my wife and I were driving along Seventh Street in Los Angeles, looking for the Don Lee Building. We found it, parked our car, and went in. The salesrooms and business offices were closed, of course, but one elevator was running, and we told the operator we wanted the studio floor. Then we walked along the spacious hallways hunting for our goal, a KHJ studio. From other studios we heard some loud and jazzy singing, so we kept on. Finally, we came to a door opening into a big room, and just inside the door we saw a big man. The sense of strangeness dropped away, for the big man had brought our hunt to an end. It was genial, big-bodied, big-hearted, big-souled Charlie Fuller. Into the studio we hurried, and then we saw Mrs. Fuller—"Grace" to Mrs. Trumbull and myself, and from both of them we had the heartiest kind of welcome. I was to see and hear for myself, that evening, something I had long known about but had not yet visited—a broadcasting service of the Old Fashioned Revival Hour.

"The studio was a large, very plain room, perhaps fifty by sixty feet. A block of seats across one side, facing the entrance, took care of about thirty people. Another block of seats at right angles with the first held about the same number; these were the choir, I learned later. There was a grand piano in a far corner, with a vibraharp in the front-center of the room. While we waited for the service to begin, and while talking with Mr. and Mrs. Fuller and other friends, four young men were standing, their heads close together, singing quietly but with perfectly trained voices some of the old gospel hymns. This was the quartet, whom I had been thrilled to hear over the air and whom I was now to hear face to face. Each one of the quartet is a consecrated Christian, and one or more of them have had tempting offers from motion picture companies, which have been declined on the ground that the Christian life, and evangelistic singing, and the motion picture profession, do not mix.

"Half a dozen microphones were distributed in different parts of the studio, Mr. Fuller's 'mike' and his reading stand being not far from the door where we had first seen him. Another microphone, a dozen feet away, was Mrs. Fuller's 'pulpit.' The rest of the 'mikes' took care of the choir, quartet, piano, and vibraharp. Still other visitors who came in from time to time were accommodated with chairs, and there must have been a hundred people present when the service was under way. But, while one hundred of us were listening or sharing in that Sunday evening service, those who were listening with us, outside the studio, numbered probably 5,000,000 souls, from California to Maine, from Florida to Alaska, as the six studio microphones carried the prayers, the hymns, the announcements, and the gospel sermon to eighty-five stations of the Mutual Broadcasting System and its affiliated stations throughout North America.

"Conversation quieted, and one could feel the atmosphere of intent, even intense waiting and anticipation, as the big electric clock in plain sight of all showed 7:28, then 7:29. But several minutes before the 'zero hour' had come, Mr. Fuller had led us all in earnest prayer for God's blessing upon the service. "God bless you. Either you are in Christ or out of Christ. God bless you, my dear man. God bless you over here. Any on the lower floor of the auditorium? Hands are going up all over. God bless you over there. In the balcony to my right? Settle it today. 'Today harden not your hearts.' In the balconies to the rear? Put your hand up and say, 'Brother Fuller, pray for me.' In the balcony to my left? Settle it today. 'Come all ye that labor and are heavy-laden.' God bless you.

"As the hands of the clock came to 7:30, and the red electric bulb gleamed out, the announcer quietly told the listening millions that the Old Fashioned Revival Hour had begun, and the choir and quartet sang the Theme Song, 'Jesus Saves.'

"As Charles Fuller spoke his opening words to his vast unseen congregation a quiet little smile of welcome was on his face and in his voice, and one felt as though he were just speaking to a little circle of intimate personal friends, instead of to an eager, continent-wide assemblage.

"He was very noticeably the commander-in-chief of his forces during the next sixty minutes. Every two or three minutes he took a look at that clock, for he knew just how much time each hymn, announcement, solo, letter-reading, and every detail should fill. His bearing was alert, electric in its responsibility and leadership. As he came near the end of what he was saying, from time to time, he raised a finger in the direction of the choir or the quartet, or the vibraharp, as a signal that they were to do their part the instant he stopped speaking. Watching the clock, he knew whether two, or three, or four verses of a hymn should be sung, and this was signaled by the lifting of one or two or more fingers. When he knew that at the end of any verse that selection should stop, he gave the extremely expressive signal of passing his fore-finger swiftly across his throat—the signal could be understood even by one who had never been in the studio before!

"The choir singing and the quartet music are a faultless part of his ministry. Leland Green, an accomplished young musician and choir leader who worked with Mr. Fuller in the Placentia church, is in charge of the Revival Hour music, and is a soloist also with the beautiful vibraharp.

"No part of the program is more eagerly awaited than Mrs. Fuller's personal message and reading from letters received. The whole program is so beautifully human, by the way; nothing stiff, or artificial, or theatrical in it, but just plain home folks talking to one another and talking to you. When Mrs. Fuller's part in the program comes, Mr. Fuller announces it, then says, 'All right, dear,' or 'Go ahead, honey,' just as though he and she were in a little group of half a dozen people instead of millions. But the millions are drawn nearer to the hearts of these dear children of God by these spontaneous, unrehearsed, touches . . .

"That God was giving the message through Charles Fuller, no one who watched and listened could doubt. His love of God, love of the Word, love of the Saviour, and love of souls burned in his heart, his voice, his face. He was not watching the clock now—clock and friends and strangers in the studio were forgotten, as God carried him through his message and held him faithful to it. He spoke from carefully prepared notes and outline, of course, and he knew, from experience, how long it would take to give the message, so it was safe for him to forget the clock. Toward the end of the sermon he glanced at the timepiece, and a few minutes later he brought his message to a close.

"And then, after prayer and hymn, the memorable service was over. When the light in the gleaming red electric bulb faded out, the first thing Mr. Fuller did was to lead all in the studio in prayer that God would bless the service just held and use it to the saving of souls."

It would be most interesting to know how many descendants, and descendants of friends of the Fuller-Day-Payton families, have themselves received blessing through the Old Fashioned Revival Hour. Only this week I received a letter from the present librarian at Vergennes, Vermont, in which she communicates the information that with her own mother, recently deceased, the Old Fashioned Revival Hour was the favorite broadcast program of the week, but that neither she nor her mother had ever dreamed that the Dr. Fuller on that broadcast was the son of Henry Fuller who in a preceding generation had built and managed an excelsior factory in that small town.

Thousands of great stories could be told of how the lives of men and women have been transformed, their whole course of living radically changed, and a new world opened to them, through the messages they have heard from one whose face they probably will never see. One among many, never before told, I happen to know from first-hand information, being the teacher of the young man involved in this remarkable, almost miraculous story. In 1938 there was living on a barren, unproductive piece of ground near Mustang, Colorado, many miles from a railroad station, an elderly couple, utterly incapable of daily work, and a grown, unmarried son, who was struggling to eke out a bare living from this almost hopeless farm, and at the same time care for his aging parents. Neither father nor son had had much education, the son having never finished grammar school. Each Sunday afternoon it was the custom of this lonely family group, far away from any large city, to tune in the Old Fashioned Revival

Hour. There came an hour when the preceding work of the Holy Spirit brought this young man to a crisis. As he listened to the message that February afternoon, on a battery-operated radio in his Ford automobile, he fell on his knees, receiving Christ, asking God to forgive his sins, and to bestow on him the gift of eternal life. A complete and glorious conversion took place there and then. It was not long before the Spirit of God began to stir up the heart of this plain, rural son to acquire some training in the Word of God, in preparation for some kind of Christian service, but he could not leave his parents, and there was no adequate means for putting them in the care of an institution where they would be comfortable and receive personal care. Five years went by, as the son kept working this unproductive ground, and caring for his parents, until the Lord took them home. Selling the land for what he could get, he came to Chicago, and went to the Moody Bible Institute to enroll as a student. When by his application it was discovered that he had never entered high school, the authorities, of course, told him that while they would like to have him, it was really against their rules to receive anyone without a high school education, and they would not be able to accept him as a student, though they recognized his earnestness and his genuine experience of regeneration.

Now it so happened that this young man had a distant relative in the city of Chicago, an outstanding Christian, with a host of friends, and out to the north side he went to see this relative and ask if he could possibly do anything to persuade the Moody Institute to receive him, even on probation, as a student. The man took him down to the office of the President, whom he knew well, and laid the case before him, presenting this proposition: "If this young man enters and is found, during the first three months, capable of getting his studies and passing the examinations, would you take him as a special student?" It was agreed that he would be so received —no one, I think, believing he could ever make the grade. I saw him myself in his early days at the Institute, and personally, I was confident that he would inevitably flunk all the examinations when they came up. After the first semester, he was still around, and occasionally I would ask him, "How are you getting along?" to which he would always reply, in his very slow drawl, "Oh, all right." Well, he passed all his early examinations, and then did an astonishing thing in changing from the regular two-year Bible course to the Pastor's Course—and that meant Greek, three years of Greek! When I heard that, I was positive he had written doom for himself. However, he was still there six months later, and I began to ask around among the other teachers as to how he was getting along. I found he was asking no favors, was being shown no favors, and was making the grade. He graduated from the Pastor's Course, being able today to read his Greek New Testament, and then felt a call to do work among the Hebrew people, and took an additional year in which he *studied Hebrew!* And that young man, from a humble hut in Colorado, because of that message on Sunday from Dr. Fuller, possesses today a better equipment for the study of the Word of God than thousands of ministers in this country, born with advantages that were never his. This fall he has accepted the pastorate of a church in a small town in Kansas.

Though it is a story of an altogether different nature, I cannot go on to talk about the later developments of the Old Fashioned Revival Hour until I record one of the most interesting, heart-moving communications that Dr. Fuller has had in his years of broadcasting. In 1943, a letter came to the Old Fashioned Revival Hour office which told this story: A woman of quite acute poverty was living in the Pecos region of Texas with her family, engaged in dry farming. She had been enjoying the Old Fashioned Revival Hour for years, and wanted so badly to send a contribution for its support, as an expression of her gratitude, but she simply did not have any money which could be contributed. One Sunday afternoon, after listening to the broadcast, she asked God if He would not provide some means, however small, which she could use for this purpose. A wind storm was then raging around her humble home, and looking out the window, she saw something fluttering in the breeze which looked like more than a mere piece of torn paper. When she went out to discover what this was flying about, she found it to be a dollar bill, which had just fallen into the clay of this famous cliche formation. Here was an answer to her prayer. She picked up the dollar bill, wrote a brief note on what appeared to be butcher paper and sent it to the office of the Old Fashioned Revival Hour. Dr. Fuller carries this dollar bill with him in his wallet everywhere he goes. Often he has told the story at great mass meetings, and he believes that possibly fifty thousand dollars has been given since 1943 to the Old Fashioned Revival Hour just through people being shown this dollar bill, still showing the clay from that Texas farm.

In 1940, Dr. Fuller's studio audience had grown so large that he undertook the rental of the great Municipal Auditorium in Long Beach for his Sunday afternoon services. A word must be said about this city which the Old Fashioned Revival Hour has made known throughout the world. Long Beach began slowly with the dreams of William Erwin Willmore, an Englishman who came to America in 1855, appearing in Southern California fifteen years later. Stopping to rest on a grass-covered plain in what is now the center of Long Beach, he decided there to establish a colony which was to be called the American Colony, and advertised his plans for developing orange, lemon, fig, and walnut groves. Somehow the scheme did not catch fire, and with only about a dozen houses being erected in two years, the plans were abandoned.

The Municipal Auditorium at Long Beach, California where the Old Fashioned Revival Hour originates each Sunday

New life came to the city, with a change of owners, and by 1888 the place was recognized as an outstanding seaside resort, twenty-three miles down the coast from Los Angeles; elegant hotels were built, and for many years no saloon was allowed inside the city limits. Here the Chautauqua held a large assembly every year. A book written in 1888 says, "The social life of Long Beach is of the kind that most delights people of refined tastes. There is nothing loud; there is much that is aesthetic; it is par excellence an educational watering place. The beach is a perfect natural race course, and during the season spanking teams from the city can always be seen dashing over this superb driveway."

By 1910, Long Beach could count 18,000 people, and by 1920, 55,000. The year after this, oil was discovered not far away, at Signal Hill, and the wells, which were soon producing more than 250,000 barrels a day brought a boom to the city, and made it leap within a few years to a metropolis of over 100,000. During the second World War, a great naval base was established near-by which handled over four million tons of cargo each year of the war. Aircraft factories sprang up which alone employed thirty thousand workers, so that by 1945 Long Beach had grown to be a city of over a quarter-million people.

The great Municipal Auditorium at Long Beach was built in 1930–1932, costing nearly three million dollars. The Convention Hall, where the Old Fashioned Revival Hour is conducted, has a seating capacity of 4,400. The amazing thing is—to the writer of this book a modern miracle of gospel preaching—Dr. Fuller preaches every Sunday afternoon week after week, year after year, in this Auditorium to never less than three thousand people, and sometimes to as many as four thousand. The service generally begins one-half hour before the broadcast itself, when announcements are made, congregational singing is entered into, a collection is taken, and audience, choir, quartet, and Dr. and Mrs. Fuller, get ready for the moment when the red light is turned on. I know the statement is a comprehensive one, but unless my knowledge of religious services in America is woefully meager, I think one is safe in saying that no man preaching in America today speaks regularly, in church or out, to between three and four thousand people *every Sunday afternoon,* fifty-two Sundays a year aside from Dr. Fuller. There is nothing spectacular about the service. The music is the finest. There is a warm, cordial, family feeling. Generally Dr. Fuller tries to ascertain the names of the states from which the audience comes each week. Often twenty-five states of the union are represented, and always a number of foreign countries, both of Europe and the continent of Asia.

I know of no sight in America offering so strong a confirmation of the truthfulness of the words of the Lord Jesus, "I, if I be lifted up, will draw all men unto me," as the one seen in the vicinity of the Municipal Auditorium of Long Beach every Sunday afternoon in the year. On both sides of the Auditorium are the great bathing beaches which have made Long Beach famous, to which in warm weather come thousands of bathers. It is not necessary here to characterize our modern bathing beaches, except to say that sometimes the beaches and streets near-by remind us of two ancient cities destroyed of God in patriarchal days. Of course, due to war work and naval operations, thousands of men in uniform, and the fact that Long Beach is a great pleasure resort, there are innumerable taverns, though the town is kept clean, without rowdiness. Straight through all this pour these thousands of people, coming in cars from three directions, north, south, and east; many visitors drive hundreds of miles to listen to one service before returning to their homes in other parts of the country. The significant thing is that, as I noticed recently, when the weather cools and the beaches are almost empty, the crowds still come. You cannot regularly do this, week after week, year after year, with any other message heard in the western world. You cannot draw three and four thousand people every week, year after year, by expounding Plato, or discussing Aristotle, or extolling the philosophy of Seneca, nor even in dramatizing the great tragedies of Shakespeare. I doubt if a Beethoven, Bach, or Wagner concert week after week, for years, would draw three or four thousand people to the same spot. One great theme magnetically pulls these hungry souls into that auditorium—the grace of God revealed in the Son of God as given to us in the Word of God.

During the spring of 1949, Dr. Fuller was approached by the ABC Network regarding the possibility of the Old Fashioned Revival Hour going out over its many stations. The complicated contract was finally signed, and ABC began carrying the Old Fashioned Revival Hour on June 19, 1949. This network now has approximately three hundred different outlets across the country, and the latest official report gives a potential audience for ABC of 33,276,000 *families*. This does not mean that the Old Fashioned Revival Hour is going out over three hundred outlets, but it is identified with a system that has that large a coverage, and the number of stations using the Old Fashioned Revival Hour continually rises. For the first time, all the broadcasts are now by transcription; the program at Long Beach on Sunday afternoon is no longer sent out direct over the air, but the hour is conducted as it has been through the preceding years, and the service of one Sunday afternoon recorded on tape or discs is used on the following Sunday from coast to coast at eight o'clock Sunday morning in each of the four standard time areas. The ABC Network, it might here be said, is an outgrowth of the older famous Blue Network of the National Broadcasting Company, having been organized as the American Broadcasting Company in July, 1943. This company is proceeding to develop a complete program of television, and perhaps someday the millions of listeners to Dr. Fuller will be able to actually see him and look into his face in their own homes.

One might ask the question as we draw to the end of this chapter: What is it that has made the Old Fashioned Revival Hour so amazingly effective? What is it that has been the means of bringing hundreds of thousands to a confession of Christ as their Saviour? What is it that draws people back on Sunday after Sunday, year after year, to their radios to hear this same man preach the same gospel? There is nothing here that we would call oratory, there are no tricks, there is nothing of a sensational nature, and there are no prizes offered. Controversial questions are seldom discussed. Yet, millions continue to listen. Well, of course, we must recognize that the first half-hour of this program contains the most wonderful gospel music to be heard anywhere in America today. As one turns the dial on Sunday to different programs, the musical part of the Old Fashioned Revival Hour is always so superior that one does not need to even make comparisons. Mrs. Fuller's reading of the letters has always proved a blessing to multitudes.

But undoubtedly the most magnetic, human aspect of all the program is the voice of Dr. Fuller. There is no voice quite like it in American preaching today. First, it is filled with pathos, with love for men and women. Some voices are harsh, some are brittle, some are mechanical, some are just natural, some are vibrant, some are rich; but Dr. Fuller's voice makes the listeners feel that he is speaking from a heart of love. One does not listen very long before he knows that the man who is speaking is in dead earnest, a man with deep convictions. He is absolutely confident of the truthfulness of the word he is uttering. He is not suggesting something; he does not debate issues; he does not, as it were, present two sides to a question, and leave the audience to decide which is right or wrong. He believes the only way men can be saved is by the gospel which he is preaching. It has saved him, it has saved great multitudes of others, he knows it is going to save men and women that day. Often even before he preaches he will give an invitation, and the very warmth of that invitation will lead fifty or sixty people to raise their hands for prayer. Then there is an urgency in Dr. Fuller's message. He believes the time is short. He knows that many who are listening to him one Sunday will not be able to listen another Sunday. "Now is the accepted time" is a motto with Dr. Fuller. There is, of course, great simplicity in his message. I have been told again and again that if one wants to write a syndicated column for any newspaper in this country, he must put his material in the simplest language, making it understandable to people who have never had more than a grammar school education. This is what Dr. Fuller does. He has great visions of work to be done, but his thinking is in simple terms, and that is the way he preaches. The profundities of theology are important, but he is not particularly interested in them. People can understand what he is saying, and of course that is a tremendous asset. All who listen to him recognize that what Dr. Fuller is saying rests upon the Word of God. He has the authority of divine revelation behind his message, and there is no authority in the world to compare with that for persuading men to make a great decision. All men know he is a voice for God. While his message is identified with the old gospel, and his program is called the Old Fashioned Revival Hour, no man is more up-to-date than he is in the relating of his message to these days, and this is principally because he has been a careful student of the prophetic Word.

Beyond all this, there rests upon his spoken utterances the mysterious, indefinable, unpurchasable power of the Holy

Spirit of God. Not only does he speak about the Son of God from the inspired pages of the Scriptures, but there rests upon him the power of the Spirit of the living God, and this is what carries the message home to the hearts of these people.

California has given birth to or has weaned more new fantastic religious cults than any other area on the continent —so many that some have called Southern California "cuckoo land." They extend from the visionary schemes of William Money in the 1870's and the Point Loma Theosophical Community, to the hopes of Mrs. Annie Besant for developing here a new race of supra-humans, and the now decaying "I Am" movement, "a witches cauldron of the inconceivable, the incredible, and the fantastic." In the midst of—and in spite of—all these humanly-conceived, man-honoring, esoteric and deceiving schemes of salvation that have never saved, great churches have been erected where the pure gospel is preached, flourishing Sunday Schools give genuine teaching of the Word of God to happy, healthy, children, real revivals are frequently witnessed, the gospel is proclaimed to hundreds of congregations, large and small, and Charles E. Fuller, for a quarter of a century, has, with these, taught people how to distinguish the true from the false, and clearly points bewildered, sin-burdened men and women to the Way of Life which leads to forgiveness, bestows Eternal Salvation, and results in peace and joy here, with the assurance of an inheritance that fadeth not away. Thus does the Light continue to shine in the darkness, "and the darkness overcomes it not" (marginal reading of John 1:5).

Chapter X

"THE SWEETEST VOICE IN AMERICA"

Every Sunday afternoon for the last twelve years, about fifteen minutes after the program has begun, the beloved director himself makes an announcement something like this: "You will now hear Mrs. Fuller read the letters. Honey, it's your turn." Sometimes he will say, "Mrs. Fuller does not want me to say this, but I am going to say it anyway. You will now listen to the sweetest voice in America." The letters she has read through the years would fill ten volumes that could well be entitled, "Modern Miracles." All those used in this chapter have been written, with one exception, within the last fifteen months, and are only a fragment, of course, of the interesting mail that comes to the Old Fashioned Revival Hour.

Probably no one group in all this quarter of a century of Dr. Fuller's broadcast has been so blessed and brought face to face with Christ as the army, navy, and marine men of our great nation. Here is a letter from the navy barracks at Miami in the midst of the second World War:

"Your program has just gone off the air, and I can say I really enjoyed every moment of it. I have listened to you under almost every circumstance in the last three years. I have been in your studio at least a dozen times, have had the car radio on while travelling cross-country, and in the last year since I have been in the navy I have heard your program in almost every port of the world.

"One program some months ago I shall never forget as long as I remember anything. We were sailing on a large troop transport ship in the Southwest Pacific. Everything was very calm, and your program had just come on the air. The men were listening very quietly, when all of a sudden the bell rang out for manning our battle stations. In the rush, the radio was not turned completely off. My battle station was directly under one of the loud speakers connected to the radio, and very faintly I could hear your choir singing. In a very short time anti-aircraft guns began their barking, and for about five minutes (which seemed like ages) my mind was drawn from your program to combat with the enemy, and I forgot it completely. But when the roar of the guns ceased, I stood quietly, and then I heard the quartet singing, very softly and plainly, 'Take Time to be Holy.' In some way it went through me like a dagger. Before I unloaded the machine gun, which I had charge of, I bowed my head and thanked God that I knew what that song meant, thanks to my godly parents. An instant later, someone turned the radio up so it could be heard by loud speaker over the ship, and instead of the usual loud discussion of the attack by all hands, everything was just as quiet as if we had been right in the studio with you. Immediately after your program the chaplain gave a five-minute talk to the men, and several gave their hearts to Christ. Some of those men are in eternity now, and how thankful we are they are spending eternity with Christ. It may interest you to know that my father is a minister of the same gospel which you preach."

From Mexico a man in the navy recently wrote:

"I have heard your gospel radio messages while on service in different parts of the world. During the cold Sundays this winter, down on the Atlantic seaboard, the messages made me warm spiritually. The sweetest and most gladdening time of all was one Sunday on the Atlantic, returning from overseas on a minesweeper, tired,

"THE SWEETEST VOICE IN AMERICA" 143

somewhat downhearted and weary, when lo and behold, your voice of cheer and comfort reached me on the 'last day warning and hope' program, for that is what I call it. I never can say what it meant to me. I have been an active Christian for over twenty-two years, and have proved it has paid dividends throughout my naval career. Men often say to me, 'How lucky you are.' I reply, 'While others take a chance, I make a choice.' "

A captain in the Alaskan Air Command tells this incident:

"It was on a Sunday night, I was sitting in the radio compartment behind the pilots' seats. We were flying at about ten thousand feet. I had turned all around the dial trying to find a worthwhile program, when suddenly at 10 P.M., I heard the strains of 'We have heard the joyful sound, Jesus saves, Jesus saves.' I nearly whooped out loud above the roar of the engines. We all listened to the entire program and I could not figure out what station was carrying it as there was no program announcement and it was on short wave. The signal was clear as a bell without a break. Imagine my joy, as we were descending to come down to our approach level at Shreveport, when at the end of the program, I heard the announcement: 'You have just listened to a transcribed broadcast of the Old Fashioned Revival Hour coming to you from Station HCJB, Quito, Equador.' "

There must be millions of sick people in the world who have had, through the Old Fashioned Revival Hour, blessing, comfort, renewed hope, and in many cases the very gift of eternal life brought to their hearts as they listened to a message they might not otherwise have heard. Two men in Tucson, Arizona, recently wrote:

"We are patients in a tuberculosis sanatorium in Tucson, and look forward each Sunday to hearing you. The weeks are so long, lying here in bed waiting for Sunday to come and bring us your program; yet when it does arrive, the hour is so short that it is gone before we know it. When your program comes on, all activity in our ward ceases—we see to that—until your voice finally fades away and is gone, and there is another long week to wait. Not until one is bedfast does he fully realize how much he really needs God. And thanks to you, Rev. Fuller, you have brought us nearer to Him. Although we can't be with you in body on Sundays, our radio is putting us bed patients, so lonely and often discouraged, right into your giant audience each Sunday, and it does so much for us. We're asking you to pray for us. Our contribution has to be small, but I hope it will help in the work for God, so that you won't have to cut off any stations, and that you will be able to keep our station!"

We could frankly speak of many of the results of the Old Fashioned Revival Hour as nothing less than miracles. One Sunday recently Mrs. Fuller read the following:

"Something very interesting happened in the state of Nebraska, and I am sure you will rejoice to hear about it. A friend of ours, who lives in Milwaukee, was holding revival meetings in Nebraska. At a service one night the Spirit of God moved a certain lady to repentance and she went to the altar, and was converted. Her husband got very angry and began abusing her on the way home, and finally told her to leave, as he didn't want her around any more. They had some distance to drive and while scolding her, he had the radio on, and the program changed to your hour. The singing quieted him, and as they traveled along the country road, the lady saying nothing, her husband listened as Mr. Fuller gave the message. The Spirit of God worked in that man's heart, and by the time they reached their home, they both got quietly out of the car. Then the man turned to his wife, his voice choked with tears and he said, 'Wife, we cannot go on like this.' She said, 'No, we can't, but you can come with me, for I am going God's way.' They knelt down together right there in the yard and the man was converted just as his wife had been a short time before. Then he, who was so mad at the evangelist, went to him the next day and said, 'Brother Carl, if you have no place to stay, you can come to our house, for you are most welcome. Now old things have passed away, and I have become a different man. From now on I am living a Christian life.' "

Missionaries all over the world have been encouraged in their work, and given messages which they can translate to their own native people, week after week, year after year. Here is one from far off Indonesia:

"For over eight years we supported the Old Fashioned Revival Hour by our prayers and regular offerings. Now as new missionaries, we are working among the mountain people near Molino, Celebes, Indonesia. For some time we have been hungry to enjoy an hour of fellowship and music around the Word again. I never dreamed I could get your program, which we have loved so long, but last night while I dialed the short wave radio, I heard the one word, 'Brother,' in a voice so familiar I was startled, for it was unmistakably your voice, Mr. Fuller. Imagine our joy to turn the dial back and be able once more to get your program, with all it means to us. Your preaching and the music were wonderful, and they came in clearly. May the Holy Spirit add to the church daily in increasing measure, through the ministry of the Old Fashioned Revival Hour. This we pray also for the Celebes."

Alaska seems to be particularly a field of great blessing. Less than a year ago Mrs. Fuller read the following from a small village in the northern part of our northern-most possession:

"We are in a village here teaching seventy-five little Eskimos. There is a small church here, founded by the Moravians, and the Eskimos hold services, speaking in their own language. We attended on our first Sunday here, and what was our joy to hear them sing, for our benefit, 'Heavenly Sunshine' in English. It is also their favorite chorus at the Eskimo school. This village is about sixty miles from the Bering Sea. The only means of travel is by plane and dog team, and mail is very irregular. We are so thankful that we can get your programs Sunday at 9 P.M., from Anchorage. It is the only gospel broadcast we can get here, but we do praise God, for it happens to be our favorite. Enclosed you find our tithe to help in keeping this station here in Alaska . . . If you could stop in the chaplain's office on Sunday evening, it would thrill your heart to hear the boys joining with you in singing 'Heavenly Sunshine' and to see their quietness and interest in hearing the message. The program has been vitally instrumental in nourishing a number of young Christians here. A former WAAC gave her testimony in chapel the other evening, saying that she was converted by her radio after hearing one of the programs. We have had some contacts with missionaries in Alaska, and noted the fine pioneer spirit which is evidenced in their work here."

We cannot help but add another from a minister in the Eskimo region of Alaska:

"The ringing notes of the Old Fashioned Revival Hour and 'Jesus Saves' were released for the first time over our station last night, into Eskimo camps all around this Arctic Coast, from Victoria Island to Alaska, to army personnel at the Loran stations, into homes and villages of Indian and white trappers, along the Mackenzie River and the upper Yukon River in Alaska. Yes, the gospel rang out here in a glorious broadcast. We have already had reports from listeners in the outlying villages, of the joy and appreciation in hearing you from Aklavik. I am sure that reports will come directly to you. May there be abundant fruit from this good seed of the gospel, as we earnestly pray the Spirit to prepare hearts to receive the Word."

And here is one from far-off Persia:

"We want you to know how very much we are enjoying hearing the broadcasts again. Of course, we listened in America, but three years ago we came overseas, to work here in the orphanage, a small independent missionary effort, right in the rugged mountains of Kurdistan. This summer we had a fine radio and wind charger sent to us by friends in the homeland. Can you imagine what it means to us to get the Old Fashioned Revival Hour clearly away over here. We certainly rejoice when we hear that program from home. Enclosed is a copy of 'Heavenly Sunshine' as I have translated it into Persian. May the Lord bless you as you shed this sunshine all over the world, by means of radio."

One would like to know, but we will not until we get to heaven, how many ministers in this country have received fresh encouragement to go on preaching the gospel, in the midst of discouragement or some subtle temptation to begin preaching some other message than the saving grace of God, through the Old Fashioned Revival Hour. A minister from Missouri, with two doctorate degrees, recently wrote:

"It has suddenly come to me that you are my pastor. Even though I am the pastor of a large congregation in this county-seat town, it is a strange paradox that the pastor doesn't have a pastor to feed his soul with God's Word and this past week I have decided that you are my pastor in that every Sunday morning, 8:30–9:30 (Central Time) over KOAM, Pittsburg, Kansas, you thrill my heart with the preaching of the gospel."

Another young pastor in Illinois has recently written:

"For ten years I have enjoyed the Old Fashioned Revival Hour, but have often wondered, 'Is it really doing the job —is it reaching the unsaved? It is fine the Christian is being strengthened. But do the lost tune in the program?' I confess I didn't think so. But in my pastoral calling to the unsaved in this, my first charge, I am amazed to find that almost everybody knows the 'Heavenly Sunshine' man. Best of all, they listen, not only to the music, but just as eagerly to the messages as well. It's the best music on the radio, I am told, and Reverend Fuller preaches the Bible so plainly and understandingly that we just can't miss it. That's what they, these unchurched, unsaved people, say to me. Yes, the Holy Spirit through your broadcast has planted the good seed and now I, as a young pastor, am privileged to come along and reap the harvest. Let me give you an example of this. Last month I was able to lead to the Lord a coal miner who had been hospitalized after being severely crushed under a rock slide. Every rib, as well as his back was broken. While under the rock he had cried out, 'God help me, for if I die now, I die in my sins.' Now this man had been a real prodigal, but in his extremity he knew he was a sinner, and he knew he needed salvation. Where had he learned this? After he was gloriously converted, I learned that even in his unsaved state he had been listening to the Old Fashioned Revival Hour, and there he had learned the way of salvation, and that the wages of sin is death. Thank God for the heart preparation your ministry has given that bore fruit in this mighty work of salvation."

"THE SWEETEST VOICE IN AMERICA" 149

On the high seas, away from one's native land, feeling conscious of strangeness and risk, so many have been blessed. This letter recently came from a man in Scotland:

> "Being a believer in Christ, I feel it is my duty to tell you how an 'Old Revival Hour' programme was a comfort to me during a hazardous journey from the Old World to the New. Many months ago I was sailing in the Atlantic, during the course of which we were being pursued by our relentless foe, an enemy U-boat. This man-made fish had caused the destruction of two of our ships; consequently, we feared the worst would happen, as we were the last one left in that area. It was my 19th birthday, and being far from those near and dear, and living in an environment of suspense, made me feel a little downhearted.
>
> "As I sat in our wireless room, my ears straining for distress signals, I heard sweet music which seemed familiar. I turned my dial so as to hear both the incoming signals. No more signals came, and to my eneffable joy, those beautiful words echoed forth in song, 'Jesus, Jesus, precious Jesus, oh for grace to trust Him more.' I have listened to your broadcast many times since, but that was the first I had ever heard, and I still maintain that was the finest birthday present I ever received."

We might take one January Sunday afternoon's letters for this year and just put them together as Mrs. Fuller read them:

> "From Michigan . . . Dear Mr. Fuller . . . We thought we would not be able to listen to your hour today, as our radio had to be taken to a repair shop, but we hated to miss it; so my husband suggested going out to the car radio, where we could hear you. Now, as you probably know, January in Michigan is far from being warm. However, we bundled up, and sat in the car the whole hour. We

must admit, outwardly we were pretty cold, but when the hour was over, we were warmed spiritually by the sermon and music, and we would gladly do it again next Sunday if it were necessary, no matter what the weather!'

"I feel that the following letter from Georgia shows a wonderful Christian spirit of love and sympathy, as this lady wrote of her feeling for the orange and vegetable growers in California, in their discouragement at the loss of their crops. While she listened to my husband's sermon, she thought what a comfort it would be to believers out here. Her letter reads: 'Your sermon of Sunday on John 4 I know was such a comfort to the people of Southern California, whose citrus and vegetable crops have been blighted and ruined by the recent unpredictable cold spell. You were showing them, Brother Fuller, that the spiritual things, not the temporal, are everlasting, and to be sought after, and that putting their trust in God and His mercy and goodness, they will be comforted.'

"This last very interesting letter is from a lady in Indiana. 'Last week my husband, who drives a truck, took a load of coal to an old blind man in a neighboring town. This old man lives all alone, and does his housework and cooking. My husband remarked about how clean he kept everything, and the old man said, "I am blind, can't see a thing, but I am not alone, for everywhere I go Jesus is with me, and He has given me an ability so that I can even count my money without making a mistake." When he counted out the money to pay for his coal, he could tell the twenty, ten and five dollar bills apart, and he counted out the change without a mistake. He said, "Twenty years ago I had cataracts on my eyes, and I went to an eye doctor, and he said he could cure me with the electric needle. But he burned the nerves in my eyes, and I have been blind ever since. Sixteen years ago I was awfully discouraged, and decided there wasn't a thing left in life for me, so I went in and felt around in the medicine cabinet for a bottle of poison I knew had been there, but I couldn't find it. So, disappointed, I wandered into the other room, and turned on the radio, and Rev. Fuller was preaching. It seems he was preaching just to me. At the end of the service, when he gave the invitation, I accepted Christ as my Saviour, and I haven't been alone since. I want you to turn on your radio at nine o'clock next Sunday and listen to Rev. Fuller—he's a Bible preacher." Well, my husband told him that he had been listening to you for years! The old man said, "That's good, Brother. I'll never see you on earth, but I hope to see you on the other side." As my husband does his trucking, he talks to a lot of people about your program, and he says it is just surprising how many people do listen to it.' "

People traveling across our country have not only often been blessed on Sunday listening to this program, but have met groups everywhere who were also enjoying the beautiful music, and the strong message from the Word of God.

"Last month I drove with some friends to Minneapolis to attend a missionary conference, and then to Seattle. Two things impressed me very much on this trip: the total absence of churches for miles and miles and miles, as we traveled by auto through Montana especially, but also Nevada and Idaho. When we stopped at gas stations, and I gave out tracts, and they saw our California license, more than once I was asked, 'Did you ever go to Long Beach, and see and hear the Old Fashioned Revival Hour?' I told them, 'Yes, indeed I have.' Then they invariably added, 'We wouldn't know how to get along without that program. It is the only church service we have out here. Why, we can hardly wait from one Sunday to another, and we love every part of the program.' Can you imagine what it would be never to have a chance to go to church? That is why people do appreciate the chance that radio gives them for fellowship and to hear the gospel."

Here is the way one Christian makes the broadcast available:

"We have a little country store here, and we open up on Sunday mornings, just so a number of people who have no radios and no chance to hear your program, or to go to any church, can come and hear. This is a poor community of mountain roads—forty miles to the nearest town. Eighteen or twenty people come every Sunday, and they sit around the stove on kegs or boxes in winter, or on the porch near the door in warm weather. We all sing the songs we know with you, and I just wish you could see the careworn faces light up as you preach. They feel they know Rudy and George, Leland and Honey, and all the rest of you, as dear friends. They don't have much but hard work and troubles, but you tell us of a better land. The good music and the messages from the Bible all mean very much to us."

A young woman working in an office in Los Angeles tells this wonderful story:

"This is just a few lines to let you know I listened to your broadcast last Sunday and was deeply touched by your sermon. It is just five years ago this month that I tuned in accidentally to your program while waiting in the city of Detroit, Michigan, to be called into active duty in the Women's Auxiliary Corps. That night what you said about eternal judgment and hell didn't suit me, and I promptly switched the dial. However, the next Sunday night I tuned again just to hear the music and singing, thinking to turn the dial when you started to preach; but when I tuned in Mrs. Fuller was reading the letters. I heard her say, 'Rev. Fuller does not tell people what they always want to hear, but he tells them the truth.' So I listened on while you preached on the first chapter of Romans. Never in all my life had I heard such a sermon. Every false foundation was swept away from under me, and I was completely changed. I rushed to my writing desk and grabbed every bit of false doctrine that was tucked away in there—false doctrines of the bloodless type, and took it down and burned it in the furnace.

"But this is just one little incident of my story. What I really want to tell you is that upon going home on my first furlough, I found my home a transformed place. The first thing I heard that first Sunday of my furlough was the Old Fashioned Revival Hour program—and could you believe it, heretofore in our home all music of a religious nature was strictly banned. And as my father and sister and I sat down to the supper table you were praying, Rev. Fuller, and they both bowed their heads and prayed along with you. Shortly after this, my elderly aunt became interested in your program, and she also got soundly converted, and my, what a change came over her. She fired so many questions at me about the Bible that I became so aware of my lack of knowledge of things spiritual that I decided to quit the army and attend Bible school. Just now I am here on the Pacific Coast doing preparatory work prior to going to China to take up orphanage work in Hong Kong. Oh, I know of so many people who have been saved listening to your broadcast I couldn't begin to mention them all."

Even members of the staff of the United Nations, writing on the United Nations stationery from Lake Success, have sent in letters telling of blessing which they have received:

"I have been meaning to write to you for some considerable time, first of all to thank you for your ministry over the air, and then to let you know what it has meant to us. My wife and I are both British and we have been in the United States for almost two years now in connection with the United Nations. Very soon after our arrival, we discovered your broadcast on our radio dial, and have been regular listeners ever since. My wife and I are both born-again Christians and your broadcasts have strengthened our faith and led us further in the knowledge of the things of the kingdom. Your ministry is quite unique, and we feel that America is indeed fortunate to have such radio programmes as yours. We have nothing quite like it in Britain, but I can well imagine what a revival would result if we had."

We cross the ocean for a moment to French Morocco, and hear Mrs. Fuller reading a letter from a navy boy stationed in North Africa, ancient site of early Christianity:

"I've heard your Scripture-filled sermons many times over the radio since I've been stationed here in French Morocco, North Africa with the navy, and love to listen to the Word as it goes out over the air. I know that thousands of people hear the gospel in places where there is no other way for them to hear it preached. I pray for you each night, and for the Word as it goes out over the air, that the Holy Spirit will work in the lives of men and women convicting them of their sin and presenting them the Saviour, our Lord Jesus Christ, the way, the truth, and the life. What a wonderful Saviour we have. I thank Him daily for the shedding of His precious blood that saves us from our sins and gives us eternal life.

"Dr. Fuller, I'm enclosing a money order and want to send you the greater part of my tithes and offerings each month to help publish the good news of the Lord Jesus Christ."

Let me close this chapter with what I think is one of the greatest stories of conversion that has come to my attention for a long time. I heard Mrs. Fuller speak of this letter as

Dr. and Mrs. Charles E. Fuller

soon as it was received, and then heard her read it in September of last year:

"I want to tell you that I have accepted Jesus Christ as my Saviour, after hearing the way of salvation when your program was on the air, and I think you would like to hear about it. I have had polio, but have never walked. One Sunday about two weeks ago, my mother and father and I were listening to some dance music. My parents decided to go visiting, so I asked them to take me out of my wheel chair, and put me to bed. After they had done that they left the house, but they forgot to turn the radio off. I lay there listening, and then heard your program when it came on. But oh, how I wanted to get up and turn that radio off, for I had decided when I was younger that I wasn't going to have anything to do with religion, for I felt that God was cruel and didn't love me, because I had to sit in a chair crippled, while other girls could go, could run and dance and have fun. Pastors had come to call on me, but I would not even listen to them, and didn't want to listen to you either, but I could not help it. I heard the music, which is so beautiful, and then I heard your sermon. It wasn't long until the tears were in my eyes, for I realized that I was a sinner, I needed God, and wanted to come to God. Right then I asked the Lord Jesus to come into my heart, and now I am so happy. Mr. Fuller, please pray that my parents will be converted. Pray that God's will may be done in my life, and that I may be healed if it is His will. How grateful I am to you for leading me to the Lord. I know I'll see you in heaven."

With a gracious personality and charm for initial assets, to which were added elocutionary gifts, and careful training, Mrs. Fuller has through these years communicated the truths and lessons of these letters to the hearts of millions with telling effectiveness.

CHAPTER XI

THE FULLER EVANGELISTIC FOUNDATION

Soon after the close of his ministry at Placentia, Dr. Fuller organized in August, 1933, the Gospel Broadcasting Association. At the present time, the President of this is the Rev. Dr. Harry MacArthur, an outstanding Baptist clergyman in the Los Angeles area. The Vice President is Dr. Henry Hutchins, for many years now the faithful pastor of the Lake Avenue Congregational Church, Pasadena, and a vital influence in the National Association of Evangelicals. Dr. Fuller himself is the Managing Director, and his faithful private secretary, who so efficiently manages the busy office on Mentor Street, Miss Rose Baessler, is the Secretary. In addition, there are twenty-five sponsors on the board of the Gospel Broadcasting Association, made up of some of the outstanding evangelical Christian laymen and ministers of Southern California. This Association is entirely devoted to one great area of activity, the work of broadcasting, which today with them means the Old Fashioned Revival Hour. With a staff of efficient office help, the Association, constantly receiving a great flow of mail, not only acknowledges all gifts sent in for the radio work, but undertakes to answer all letters of inquiry, giving especial attention to letters in which real problems are communicated. Mr. C. B. Whitwell, formerly with the Foundation, now devotes almost all of his time to the answering of the more difficult letters of inquiry, a work he is richly gifted for undertaking. An enormous amount of mail is sent out every month, including a four-page printed communication

THE FULLER EVANGELISTIC FOUNDATION 157

from Dr. Fuller himself, and to all who ask for them, lessons on prophecy, or other subjects about which Dr. Fuller might be speaking.

The Fuller Evangelistic Foundation is wholly distinct from the Gospel Broadcasting Association, and was founded January 6, 1943. Of this incorporated body, Dr. Fuller is the President, Dr. Henry Hutchins the first Vice President, Dr. Harry MacArthur, second Vice President, and Mrs. Charles E. Fuller, the Secretary. The Fuller Evangelistic Foundation probably maintains more definitely Christian evangelical work in North America than any other organization of its kind at the present time. It is from the resources of the Foundation that funds are available for the Fuller Theological Seminary, of which we will write more fully in a subsequent chapter. The Foundation also supports a remarkable group of evangelists who are continually out in the field holding evangelistic meetings, of which we will speak in a moment. There is also a juvenile worker, the Rev. Edward Bateman, who travels from one end of the country to the other engaging in work in institutions devoted to juvenile correction. Recently a Children's Department was established, which, among other things, initiates and conducts Daily Vacation Bible Schools in out-of-the-way communities, which otherwise would not be provided with such a testimony in the summer season. Last year the Foundation's workers conducted over two hundred and fifty Daily Vacation Bible Schools during which time, by very careful count, over three thousand boys and girls were led to accept the Lord Jesus Christ.

Both of these organizations, the Gospel Broadcasting Association and the Fuller Evangelistic Foundation, are registered religious non-profit corporations in the State of California, and are subject to the very strict (justifiably so) control of both state and federal authorities. Their books are open for examination by accredited state and national officers at any time. Recently, when examiners finished going over the books of the Association they remarked to Dr. Fuller, "If all corporations had their books in the shape we find those at the Gospel Broadcasting Association, there would be little work for us to do. This is the cleanest organization of its kind we have seen. You will never be subjected again to as thorough an examination as we have given you these last few weeks." It is now time to turn to one of the great departments of the Fuller Evangelistic Foundation, that of evangelizing.

Many an evangelist has been heard to say at one time or another, "Oh if I could just be in five places at one time. There are so many open doors and one can only enter one of them at a time, so many needy fields which I will never be able to reach." Dr. Fuller realized long ago that he could not carry on his great radio ministry, direct the business affairs of the Foundation, keep up with his correspondence, *and* in addition to all this, try to hold extensive evangelistic campaigns. In fact, he knew he must not be absent from home any Sunday, unless for the greatest emergency. So, in 1944, with this constant urge in his heart to get out the Gospel he developed a Department of Evangelism as a part of the work of the Fuller Evangelistic Foundation, the purpose of which was to send out evangelists into any field that needed them, but especially to areas where an ordinary evangelist could not be expected to work. This department began to function in 1945. The author of this volume has written to each of the men now in the field doing evangelistic work, asking them for personal letters concerning their ministry and this chapter will be made up entirely of their deeply appreciated and truly refreshing communications.

First of all, we should hear from the Rev. Ralph E. Mucher, the Eastern Field Director: "First, as to a survey of my own

THE FULLER EVANGELISTIC FOUNDATION 159

work, it is my privilege and responsibility as Eastern Field Director of the Foundation to cover the territory east of the Rockies from Florida into Canada. The Lord has been pleased to bless this ministry since my association with the Foundation in January of 1946, and now I have nine evangelists for whom I do all advance work. The handling of details in arranging for suitable dates between the local church and the evangelists goes through my office. The leads from the various churches either come through inquiry to the California office or personal contacts I make as I travel, and then again, half of them, I should say, as results of meetings our own men have been privileged to conduct. I have tried to visit each local church prior to the meetings to counsel with them regarding spiritual preparation, such as prayer groups, classes in soul winning, and challenging them with their opportunity and responsibility during their special meetings. We also offer some helpful suggestions as to advertising, entertainment of the evangelist, handling of the finances and many other details that should be cared for before the meetings begin. I try to keep the evangelist informed as to the picture of each church so that when he comes on the field he is not a stranger to the pastor or his group of people.

"Several months after the meetings have been finished, I contact the pastor either personally or through correspondence and get his reaction to the meetings; also, make inquiry as to the converts who made profession during this special series of meetings. I find this continued interest in the local church means much to pastor and people, and serves to encourage them in making special efforts to win men to Christ.

"I thought this would be of worthwhile information for the public to know, that I have had numbers of pastors say to me after we have had meetings, 'We praise God for the Fuller Evangelistic Foundation in enabling us to contact an evangelist who is true to the Word, a gifted preacher, and who brings a real Gospel message without riding any special hobby.' Then again, I have had pastors say, 'I am so pleased with the financial arrangement of the Foundation. It enables us to urge our people to give their money which, in a sense, is appreciation to God for the ministry of the particular evangelist and also helps our people to have a missionary vision in this great work of evangelism.'

"I quote from a letter received today: 'We feel certain that the Fuller Evangelistic Foundation is the greatest thing that has come to the field of evangelism for some time. It is greatly needed.' These are the words from a pastor of a church in western Pennsylvania, where we have just finished a series of meetings. The size of the crowd became so great that they were forced to move their meeting to another church with a larger auditorium. There were over one hundred professions of faith in Christ from this series of meetings and the pastor writes: 'I have had several more conversions as a result of the work done during the special campaign.' "

One man writes in that he has been in the following states in one year: North Carolina, New York, Ohio, Michigan, Alabama, Maryland, Indiana, and before the year is out will be in Pennsylvania, Tennessee, and Georgia. As a good summary of one man's work I would like to quote the following complete letter from one of the sixteen evangelists now laboring in the field: "I have been working with the Foundation since January, 1945.

"My work has been largely with small churches that ordinarily would find it very difficult to have an evangelist come in for a series of meetings. So during the past four and a half years the Lord has given me the privilege of seeing many small churches built up in Revival spirit as well as in attendance, both in the Church and Sunday School. In practically every series of meetings I conduct a Sunshine Club for boys and girls in the afternoons. Thus, we reach and evangelize many boys and girls not attending Sunday School. At the close of these meetings many of them become regular members of the Sunday School and Church. However, the most distinctive feature of my Sunshine Club work has been that of reaching the parents through the work done in the hearts and lives of the children.

"Since I use a trailer and car some of my time is spent in out-of-the-way places—some of them not even having a Sunday School.

"I think of Imlay, Nevada, a railroad town of between four and five hundred population. Three summers ago when my family and I were traveling through that section of the country we had an open week in our schedule that we could give to some community. We stopped to see what Imlay had in the way of churches, found they had none and that the Sunday School had been closed three months before due to lack of interest. The former Superintendent and the Secretary of the Sunday School did not feel there would be any use in trying to conduct a meeting. However, we felt led of the Lord to suggest that if we could have the use of the school building we would like to try for a few days to see what could be done. The next morning with very little advertising we had nineteen boys and girls present for the Sunshine Club. The following morning thirty-eight, and from then on, between forty and fifty in attendance. The second day we started evening services—attendance on the part of the adults was just fair, but kept building up until the closing night the schoolroom was filled. That night three or four of the adults took Christ as Saviour, several others publicly confessed Christ as their Saviour and some others came back to Christ. In the Sunshine Club twenty-seven of the boys and girls (several of them high school age) professed faith in Christ.

"A number of our meetings in California, Nevada, and Colorado have resulted in churches being established.

"We could tell about many interesting conversions, drunkards and prostitutes as well as the up-and-outers.

"All of this work that we so enjoy and that we feel the Lord laid on our hearts years ago, has been made possible through the Fuller Evangelistic Foundation. We thank God with overflowing hearts for the privilege of serving with the Foundation."

That the advance work of which Mr. Mucher speaks proves effective, let me take two paragraphs from one of the most successful of this evangelistic band, as he writes, voluntarily, concerning the preparation made for the meetings in which he has been engaged: "I came to the Foundation in March, 1948, after six full years as an independent evangelist. I must confess that I enjoyed my independent status in which the Lord was blessing abundantly. My brother, Elmer's, happy association and fellowship with the Foundation was naturally a strong and favorable influence in that direction. But I prayed earnestly for three full weeks before the Lord definitely spoke to my heart and revealed to me that it was His will for me to associate myself with the Foundation.

"I can say with simple honesty that my joy in the fellowship is increasing constantly. To me, there are many definite and blessed advantages in belonging to the Foundation. To be associated with Dr. Fuller in any capacity gives one a solid acceptance with the Christian public. I find that I am received in the utmost confidence and that previous period of break down and get acquainted is unnecessary. The constructive financial policy is perhaps the biggest advantage of all. No church suffers financially when they employ a Foundation evangelist. No Foundation evangelist can be accused of putting on pressure for finances nor can they say that any of

THE FULLER EVANGELISTIC FOUNDATION 163

them took a huge offering home with him. The giving is to the cause of Christ in general as represented by the work of the Foundation and this has a most wholesome effect. It might be interesting to you to know that prior to coming with the Foundation, I was told by some well known Christian leaders and evangelists that my offerings would decrease if I were to join the organization. I'm glad to report that my offerings have shown a decided increase during my first year with the Foundation."

One could give scores of most interesting anecdotes and experiences of these devoted servants of God, but space will allow for only a few. Here is a good testimony concerning the conversion of Indians: " 'We have never seen an Indian go forward to publicly accept Christ' was the testimony of some of the residents of an Indian Reservation in Southern California. During the afternoon meetings for children, it was soon found the Indian young people were the most alert of any group we had seen. Several confessed Christ as Saviour, but at the evening services not a single one responded until next to the last day. Then, very deliberately, three adult Indians came to the front to publicly confess Christ as Saviour. I noticed one whose face was beaded with perspiration, showing the terrific effort that it had required. But the ice was broken in the little Moravian Mission, and two others came at the next service, and one more at the final service making a total of six. 'The gospel is the power of God unto salvation to *everyone* that believeth.' "

One man was able by a single message to prevent almost an entire congregation from drifting into modernism. "Just very recently in writing to a pastor before going to his church, I felt led to say that I would be speaking on the Virgin birth of Christ. I had never begun a campaign with this subject and wondered about the wisdom of it. I arrived at the church just in time for the service on Sunday morning with no chance to talk to the pastor about the meeting. After the service the young pastor with tears in his eyes said, 'Brother, God led you to preach that message.' He had a well educated, influential man in his congregation who was arguing that Jesus is the son of Joseph, and that the Spirit had led Joseph; therefore, the birth of Christ out of wedlock was no sin. He had influenced many in the church and they were giving the young pastor a lot of trouble. After my message the man came only one more time, but the rest of the congregation was convinced that Jesus is the Son of God and a revival and Bible study broke out among the members though there were not many souls saved in the meeting."

"In Wyoming," one of the evangelists writes, "we enrolled close to 200 children in children's meetings and the pastor became jealous. In his jealousy he was blocking the offering for the Foundation in a very subtle way. But at the last children's meeting the boys and girls spied the offering envelopes and every child took one off the table. Of course, we had not said anything about their taking them, neither did I try to stop them. Then on Sunday evening it touched our hearts to see those boys and girls come with their offering of pennies, nickles, and dimes. It touched the congregation so that they gave one of the largest offerings we received that year. The last good-bye I had with the surprised pastor he was still remarking about the unusual offering."

One of the evangelists seems to be unusually successful in being the instrument of God for bringing to Christ men who have for years resisted Him. He writes: "In May, 1946, I was conducting a meeting in the Methodist Church of Rogersville, Pa. Soon after I arrived a certain man was pointed out to me as one of the hardest sinners in town. I was told that he had sat through over forty years of revival meetings in that section. All this time he had stedfastly refused Christ. We immediately set to work praying daily for him. Many even were burdened to tears over his lost soul, including his wife. He came often but would not yield. On the last night the church was crowded, and he sat through the entire service and invitation. After pleading again with the people to come to Christ we began the last verse. I saw this hardened sinner break completely down, and shaking like a leaf and weeping loudly he stumbled to the altar rail. He was gloriously saved that night with five or six other men who followed him to the front. He is now a leader in that church. This was an outstanding victory.

"A few years ago while holding a one-week series of services in the Sandusky Street Baptist Church, Pittsburg, Pa., something very unusual happened. The final Sunday morning I was speaking on the necessity of the new birth when the Holy Spirit came mightily upon us. At the invitation call along with others came two elderly ladies to the inquiry room. In the room that morning I heard one of these ladies say, 'I have been a member of this church forty years, but I have never known what it was to be born again till this morning.' The other one stood and testified, 'I was baptized in this church when I was fourteen years old, but I was never saved. This morning I have found Christ.' These testimonies were given amid tears of repentance and joy. I shall never forget the rejoicing there was among us that day."

Many of those who either are saved in these evangelistic meetings or are led to rededication ultimately go into Christian work. From the letter of one evangelist alone the following illustrations of this may be taken: "From a small church in Washington a middle-aged man sold his restaurant, went to an excellent Bible School, and is now in charge of the kitchen of a large Indian Mission on the Yukon.

"From a two-day Bible conference in a farmhouse some miles north of Anchorage, Alaska, a young woman in the despair of thinking she had missed her opportunity to take

Bible training, went to a Bible School and is now preparing for Christian service.

"From a recent evangelistic campaign a young man and his wife, esteemed in their community, came to the Lord with many tears. They are now entering Moody Bible Institute. And, the young pastor, a Bible School graduate now studying for his bachelor's degree, is now making application to enter later on Fuller Theological Seminary. From small, out-of-the-way places, where evangelists cannot make expenses, go volunteers for the foreign mission fields."

Probably some of the greatest evangelistic meetings ever conducted by the members of the Fuller Evangelistic group were those held this year, in Pennsylvania, by an evangelist who has been with the Foundation only about fourteen months, after six successful years as an independent evangelist. "This year so far I have witnessed," he writes, "the two greatest campaigns I have ever seen in my life, am about to conclude a third, have preached to more than twenty thousand people, have seen over three hundred accept Christ as Saviour while more than twelve hundred have yielded anew to God. In other words, God is blessing and this should be the greatest year ever. Praise God for the Fuller Foundation.

"The two great campaigns to which I refer were first the wonderful Connellsville, Pa., meeting which newspaper editors, pastor and people called the greatest single church revival in the history of the city. There were over four hundred decisions for Christ, including the consecrations. The Richfield, Pa., meeting, was even greater. What began as a Mennonite meeting in Richfield caught flame immediately and swept to a county-wide meeting with eight churches cooperating in a spontaneous revival that swept one hundred and thirty-six souls into the family of God, while about five hundred others made decisions for Christ. In both places people were turned away for lack of accom-

THE FULLER EVANGELISTIC FOUNDATION

modations. A total of six thousand people attended the Connellsville meeting, while over ten thousand attended the Richfield meeting."

In 1945 the Foundation supported ten evangelists in addition to three song leaders. In 1948 there were sixteen evangelists and one song leader. In the four years, 1945–48, six hundred and eleven meetings have been held, by the means of which nine thousand, three hundred and eighty-six people have been lead to receive Christ as their Saviour and eight thousand, four hundred have made other decisions of one kind or another. In addition to this, the three members of the Bible Conference Staff have in the last three years held one hundred and eighty different Bible conferences. Or to put it another way, in the years 1946, 1947 and 1948 the Fuller Foundation alone has been responsible for seven hundred and ten evangelistic meetings and Bible conferences. What a wonderful and glorious and eternally fruitful way in which to use the Lord's money! Double, treble times this number of men could be used in our land—yes, twenty times as many, if other men with some abundance of the Lord's money would undertake such definite work as this.

Chapter XII

GREAT MASS MEETINGS

There is a passage in St. Matthew's account of the early ministry of John the Baptist that has always fascinated me, "Then went out unto him Jerusalem and all Judea, and all the region round about Jordan." Imagine a man going out into the wilderness and beginning to preach, and as soon as he does, great multitudes of people from all over the adjacent country, and from the great city of Jerusalem flock to hear him. Some men can go right into the middle of a great city, in fact, into a great church, without many coming to hear them. What makes people in great crowds come to hear the simple preaching of the gospel from certain men? Some years ago, James Stalker in commenting on this passage said, "Speak the right word, and you will not need to press men to come and hear it. No obstacles can keep people away when a voice sufficiently charged with the Holy Ghost is heard." Perhaps the late Professor Stalker has the right phrase, "a voice sufficiently charged with the Holy Ghost," for it is certainly true that there are many faithful preachers of the gospel in America today, living holy lives, with a good knowledge of the Word, who do not draw great crowds. But God has given something to Dr. Fuller which not only draws millions every Lord's Day to the radio to hear the Old Fashioned Revival Hour, and to drink in the water of the Word of Life, but which also, as the years have again and again shown, has drawn people long distances to hear and see him personally. This is not only true at Long Beach every Sunday, where the Old Fashioned Revival Hour originates, but it has been true in Canada and in the United States, from the Atlantic to the Pacific, and from the Gulf of Mexico to New England.

I can remember twelve years ago when Dr. Fuller was brought to Chicago to speak for the Christian Business Men's Committee at the Civic Opera House, where six thousand people came to hear him speak, and especially the following year, when on Easter Sunday morning he spoke to forty thousand people gathered together at Soldier's Field, Chicago, which, if I am not mistaken, is the largest gathering ever held on Easter morning at that place. I was not privileged to hear Dr. Fuller on these occasions, but many of my friends did, and it seemed to me that the whole city of Chicago throbbed with new spiritual life for days after that great Easter Sunrise Service. People spoke for weeks ahead of their anticipation of hearing the one who had been bringing such blessing to their hearts with the Old Fashioned Revival Hour, and they spoke for a long time afterward of the fulfillment of that anticipation in the Easter morning service. This has been repeated again and again all over the North American continent.

Two remarkable incidents of the earlier years of these mass meetings must be mentioned in this biography, though they have been spoken of often before, and one of them, I think, has frequently appeared in print. In September, 1938, more than ten thousand people, on a day of wretched weather, gathered together in two different services at the Hippodrome in Waterloo, Iowa, a building that unfortunately for what was about to happen, had a corrugated iron roof. After a drizzling rain throughout the day, just as the evening service was about to begin, a good Iowa storm burst over that city, and the rain came down in torrents. Dr. Fuller knew that if the rain continued, two things were inevitable: first, he could not be heard, no matter what mechanical devices were being used, by the people who had gathered together in that building; and, secondly, it would not be possible to carry that service through the air, by broadcast, to the other parts of the nation. When he picked up the earphones to listen to the musical part of the program that was to precede the message, nothing could be heard but a roar, and everyone who has listened to a radio knows that if all you can hear on a program is a roar, you are going to cut it off before one full moment passes. If God wanted that service to continue, and be blessed, the rain must stop. But Dr. Fuller did not leave the matter automatically in the Lord's hands: the Scriptures never tell us to indifferently fold our arms and make no requests of the Lord. St. James says, "Ye have not because ye ask not." Dr. Fuller felt divinely led to ask God, in public prayer, to stop the rain. As he stepped to the pulpit to beckon to the great audience to be silent, while he led in prayer, the Evil One whispered to him, "Suppose the rain does not stop after you pray; they will laugh you out of town." Lifting his hand and asking the audience to join with him in prayer, he uttered these simple words, "Father, in Jesus name will you please stop the rain that this broadcast may go out clearly for Thy Glory." Dr. Fuller has often told me that it was as though a faucet was being turned off, so quickly did the rain stop, all within less than a minute, when not a drop could be heard falling on that roof. God answered prayer; He has done it for others, He did it for Charles Fuller. I do not believe that every time it rains a minister is called upon, even in an auditorium with an iron roof, to ask God to stop the rain, but when one is divinely led to offer such a prayer, one may expect the prayer to be answered. I am told that as the rain stopped, the faces of people went white with sheer fear, knowing that God was there, and when the invitation was given, Dr. Fuller tells how the people actually *ran down the aisle* to accept the Lord Jesus Christ. They had not asked for signs that night, but they got a sign, and acted upon it. Now the amazing thing is that not another drop of rain fell during the whole of the broadcast program. The benediction had been pronounced, people were talking in groups, some were going out to their cars, when again the torrents of rain fell, and so great was the downpour that for some time the people could not leave that auditorium unless they were willing to be drenched going to their cars or busses.

The following night, Dr. Fuller was to speak at Cedar Rapids. Unknown to him, the news of the act of God at Waterloo preceded him. When he went down to the church at seven o'clock, for the service to begin a half-hour later, he found the sidewalks crowded with lines of people waiting to get in. He thought that the caretaker of the church had forgotten about the meeting, and that these people were compelled by some man's carelessness to stand out in the street waiting for the doors of the church to be opened. Upon inquiring of some people standing near, he was told that the church had been opened for an hour and was already crowded to the last seat, and these people were still waiting to hear Dr. Fuller's voice over the loud speaker. Now people can say that one should not be swept off his feet, or urged to accept Christ, because of such a miracle, but, so long as the act is honest and honorable, whether it be a miracle or no miracle, whether a man be frightened until his face is white, or is quiet in his own soul, any way, so long as his heart is opened to the gospel, and the Holy Spirit can do His regenerating work, we must commend all such experiences.

Great meetings were held in New England in the spring of 1939, especially two meetings, in May, in Mechanics Building, in Boston. After the last evening meeting, a man stepped up to Dr. Fuller and gave this remarkable story: "Mr. Fuller, I am a professional gambler. One Sunday when I was in a gambling den your broadcast of two weeks ago was filling the room. I had just made $1500 and was gathering up the gains of the day when I was arrested by your gospel message. Normally I would have turned it off, but some of the songs were those my mother had sung, and somehow they laid hold of my heart that day. My gambling friends were about to turn the radio off, but I told them to leave it on. Soon we stopped playing cards, and right after that, in that very room, all the blackness and wickedness of my heart was revealed to me, and there and then I received the Lord Jesus Christ as my Saviour. Pushing the $1500 I had won across the table, I said, 'Boys, you can take it, I am through with all this,' and I walked out. I have started a new life and am confident I shall meet my mother in heaven." Hearing the Fullers were in Boston, he had to come to see the one whom God had used to save his soul. There are thousands of others like this. What a library it would make—just the stories of the conversions of those who have been saved through the Old Fashioned Revival Hour!

There came a time when Dr. Fuller found that holding these great mass meetings, and flying about the country in planes, in addition to keeping up the Old Fashioned Revival Hour, with all the burdens involved, was taxing his strength beyond normal limits, and for a while he was compelled to give up such meetings. However, invitations continued to pour in, and in 1946, he began taking a few engagements along the Pacific Coast. On September 11 of that year, ten thousand people gathered to hear him at the Civic Auditorium in Seattle, coming from as far as Yakima, Aberdeen, and Olympia; eight thousand were seated in the auditorium and two thousand gathered on the outside. The *Seattle Post Intelligencer* said, "In a voice rich with sincerity and emotion, Dr. Fuller told the story of his 'joining the ranks of those working for Christ.' "

On Tuesday, September 10, 1946, Dr. Fuller spoke to 8500 people at a Youth for Christ Rally in the Hastings Park Forum in Vancouver, British Columbia. The *Vancouver Herald* spoke of him as "folksy, silver-haired Dr. Fuller." The

Dr. Fuller holding a new little Friend in his Arms after the Broadcast at Portland, Oregon

GREAT MASS MEETINGS 173

great audience had come from Frazer Valley and American border towns. The service was supported by a 200-voice young people's choir, the Old Fashioned Revival Hour quartet, and the Salvation Army Band. It is difficult in some of these Canadian cities to get a fair newspaper report of a real evangelistic service, some of the reporters taking the opportunity to ridicule any weeping in the audience, or the coming forward of any young men to confess their sins. They all reported one sentence of the evangelist: "I do not know why God took me off an orange ranch and put me in front of this microphone, and I don't claim to be a good preacher, but I defy any preacher to preach a better gospel than I do." He began the meeting by asking the question, "How many of you were raised under a kerosene lamp?" and when a great number raised their hands, he said, "Ah, I knew there was something I liked about you folks." He seemed to especially strike out at this meeting against cocktail drinking, and cigarette smoking on the part of women, thanking God that his mother was not a person of this type. About thirty people accepted Christ at this meeting.

On Wednesday evening, November 13, Dr. Fuller spoke to a great gathering at Maple Leaf Gardens in Toronto, with the Rev. Charles B. Templeton of Avenue Road Church of the Nazarene in charge. A great crowd had gathered as early as 6:30 that evening, and as usual when Dr. Fuller spoke in Canada, the great auditorium was full by the time he was ready to speak—old people, young people, and many ministers being present. I do not know if the *Toronto Telegram* sympathetically or critically reported an incident Dr. Fuller spoke about, but we can repeat it here sympathetically: "He related how he had been attracted by an elderly man and a young woman on the plane en route to Toronto. The man was weeping and the young woman was trying to console him. Eventually the man turned to Mr. Fuller who was sitting directly across the aisle of the plane. In the course of conversation, Mr. Fuller learned that the man had just met his daughter from France. He had not seen her for many years. She had been a prisoner of the Germans. 'That man told me that before he met his daughter, he had been to the priest to confess his sins but he admitted that there was something lacking, that he did not feel right,' Mr. Fuller said. He told the distraught father that there is no one to confess your sins to but God, that no human being has any right to hear confession. The man asked him to pray for him and he did so. Then he saw what a great change had taken place in the stranger. 'The gospel of Christ is able to not only change lives but it also gives a new outlook and a new slant on life,' the evangelist declared."

The following spring Dr. Fuller was again in Canada, and addressed an audience of 7000 people gathered in the Arena of Calgary, Alberta, Tuesday night, April 8, 1947. A crowd began gathering at six o'clock, the doors were opened at 6:30, and the place was filled before the meeting began, one-third of the audience being from outside the city. Here Dr. Fuller told the story of his conversion, which has blessed the hearts of thousands of people and brought many to accept Christ. The Salvation Army Band was of great help in this meeting, as it often has been in Dr. Fuller's meetings in Canada. The *Calgary Herald* aptly said, "Dr. Fuller's platform personality is as homey as a fireplace." As often in other meetings, the evangelist warned people of the tragedy that awaited those who reject the gospel of a crucified Redeemer, and urged his great audience to seriously consider the fact that many phophecies in the Word of God were now having remarkable fulfillment, indicating that the day of the Lord's return was near at hand.

At Edmonton, Alberta, on the evening of April 9, 1947, Dr. Fuller addressed a mass meeting in the Arena, under the auspices of the Edmonton Christian Business Men's Association, when Premier Manning of Canada graciously presided.

GREAT MASS MEETINGS 175

In 1947, at the time the seminary was founded, Dr. Fuller felt again the ebbing of strength, and though he had scheduled some twenty city-meetings throughout the country, he felt under divine compulsion to cancel them all, or else come to the place where exhaustion could lead into a complete breakdown, which is the one thing a man at any time of life should try to avoid. Once in a while a large meeting is still taken, the last being in St. Louis, April 10, 1949, when a vast audience filled Convention Hall of the Municipal Auditorium, with a choir of one thousand voices, including two hundred soldiers from Jefferson Barracks.

I think it would be no more than right to close this chapter with a word concerning some meetings which Dr. Fuller's son, Dan, held this past summer of 1949. With Mr. Bob Pierce, and a party including singers, two meetings were held in Des Moines, on Memorial Day, in the ball park, one in Cedar Rapids in the Civic Auditorium, and one in the Band Shell, on the first day of June in Sioux City, where two thousand people attended each of these two meetings. In the middle of June Dan went to Alberta for four meetings at Calgary, Wetaskiwin, Edmonton, and Lethbridge. In each of these meetings, he brought a greeting from his father, and in one of them, he preached himself. The total attendance for these four meetings was seventeen thousand, with probably about three hundred definite conversions. Dan himself has written, saying, "This was not a trip in which I was following in the footsteps of my father, in mass evangelism, for I do not have any evidence yet that I have the gift of an evangelist. Bob Pierce was the evangelist on these trips; I simply went along to represent my father." Many a minister in this country, and many an evangelist, would count it the greatest joy of life if his son would just follow in the steps of his father. Many will remember hearing Dr. Fuller say himself, over the radio a few months ago, "If my own son were not a Christian today, I would not be here preaching to you."

CHAPTER XIII

FULLER THEOLOGICAL SEMINARY

When our Lord declared to men, "Ye shall know the truth and the truth shall make you free," He forever stamped the Christian church which He was to found as an institution which must advance the knowledge of men and women, advocate the constant search for the truth, and encourage the investigation of facts. He called Himself the Truth and asked the pointed question, "If I speak the truth, why do ye not believe me?" The records of our faith are forever inscribed in a book called by a name, *Bible*, which means "book." In fact, the Gospels open with the phrase, "*The book of* the generations of Jesus Christ," and conclude with the remarkable phrase, "the books that should be written." The book of Acts opens with St. Luke talking about the former treatise which he had written. Paul's epistles close with his request that his books and parchments be brought to him in the dungeon in Rome. Certainly one of the great orders definitely instituted for the Christian church is that of *teacher*. Our Lord in His great commission commanded His disciples to go and *teach* all nations, and the Spirit of God Himself has set apart in every age men who have gifts for teaching. The great Apostle Paul who laid the foundations as it were for Christian theology, was himself a scholar trained in the best rabbinical schools of his day. From the beginning the spread of the Gospel was accompanied by the establishment of educational institutions. In a very early period a seminary of great repute was established in Alexandria, for the training of candidates for the Christian ministry in which Clement of Alexandria, Origen, and others taught, which sent forth scholars to the uttermost ends of the earth. Both Eusebius and Jerome state that this school had enjoyed a succession of teachers from the time of Mark the Evangelist. Similar schools were established at Rome, Caesarea, and Antioch. Straight down through the ages has the Christian church not only encouraged but required educational institutions.

The Apostle Paul himself gives us the magna charta for such institutions: writing his last letter to his son in the faith, Timothy, he said, "Thou, therefore, my child, be strengthened in the grace that is in Christ Jesus. And the things which thou hast heard from me among many witnesses, the same commit thou to faithful men who shall be able to teach others also" (2 Timothy 2:1 and 2). The learned Dr. Alford Plummer, Master of University College, Durham, in his great work on the Pastoral Epistles, has some words that may well be placed at the beginning of our chapter: "Timothy, before leaving his flock in order to visit his spiritual father and friend, is to secure the establishment of apostolic tradition. And in order to do this, he is to establish a school,—a school of picked scholars intelligent enough to appreciate and trustworthy enough to preserve all that has been handed down from Christ and His apostles respecting the essentials of the Christian faith. There is only one Gospel,— that which the apostles have preached ever since the ascension. A second Gospel is an impossibility. This is the Gospel which has been committed to Timothy's charge. . . . The Gospel cannot be superseded by any announcement possessing a larger measure of truth and authority. So far as the present dispensation goes, its claims are absolute and final. But it may be seriously misunderstood; it may be corrupted by large admixture of error; it may be partly or even totally forgotten; it may be supplanted by some meretricious counterfeit. . . . This precious legacy which Timothy holds in trust, he in his turn is to commit to the keeping of trustworthy persons who will know its value and be capable of preserving it intact and of handing it on to others as trustworthy as themselves. . . . This then may be considered as the earliest trace of the formation of *a theological school,*—a school which has for its object not merely the instruction of the ignorant but the protection and maintenance of a definite body of doctrine."

Probably in no other country in the world, at least since the Middle Ages, have the schools of higher learning sprung so directly from the church of Christ and its desire to have an educated ministry as in America. In the original Rules and Precepts for Harvard College, 1643, we read: "Let every Student be plainly instructed and earnestly pressed to consider well the main end of his life and studies is, to know God, and Jesus Christ, which is eternal life. John 17:3. And therefore to lay Christ in the bottom, as the only foundation of all sound knowledge and Learning." The advertisement for Columbia University, then Kings College, appearing in the New York *Gazette,* June 3, 1752, reads: "The chief thing that is aimed at in this college is to teach and engage the Children to *know God in Jesus Christ,* and to love and serve him, in all *Sobriety, Godliness,* and *Righteousness* of life, with a *perfect heart, and a willing mind."* Everyone agrees that the first objective in founding our great early collegiate institutions was the adequate training of Christian ministers. President Thomas Clap in 1753 in his famous *Annals or Histories of Yale College,* wrote: "That one principal End proposed in erecting the college was to supply the Churches in the Colony with a learned pious and orthodox Ministry; to which End it was requisite that the Students of the College have the best Instructions in Divinity and the best Patterns of Preaching set before them. And that the Settling a Learned Pious, and Orthodox Professor of Divinity in the College would greatly tend to promote that good End and Design."

FULLER THEOLOGICAL SEMINARY

For some years the idea of establishing an institution for the training of gifted young men for the preaching of the Gospel in this country (and around the world) for a ministry emphatically marked by a profound knowledge of and the deepest devotion to the Holy Scriptures had been maturing in the mind of Dr. Charles E. Fuller. Before we enter upon the fascinating story of how the Fuller Theological Seminary came into being, it might be interesting to consider for a moment the relationship of evangelism and revivals to theological seminaries and schools for training clergymen and missionaries, which as far as I know has not been given the consideration it deserves. Because of the particular ministry of the founder of this seminary, a life devoted exclusively to evangelism, the subject warrants some further treatment. One would surmise, upon first thought, that any community enjoying the experience of a true revival of religion would be inclined to give little weight to the tedious, prolonged academic training of Christian ministers, believing that the power of the Holy Spirit is not limited to those who are educated (and in this they would be right) and that there would be a great danger in long years of devotion to scholastic pursuits that the religious fervor kindled in the hearts of young ministers might be subdued or snuffed out, a criticism, that has at times been justified. Nevertheless, the facts of the history of the church, and nowhere so emphatically as in our own land, all support the thesis that *many of our most notable theological seminaries have been born out of a revival,* many of them have experienced profound quickenings in revivals, and many have made vital contributions to the great revivals that have blessed our land for the last two centuries. Of the early history of Yale College, even before there was a separate theological department, the outstanding authority in this country on the history of Yale Divinity School has recently written, "A second influence favorable to the establishment of theological seminaries, particularly at Yale College, was the awakening of the churches to a new life beginning about 1734. The low state to which religion had fallen prior to the preaching of Jonathan Edwards upon Justification by Faith in Northampton in this year and the leadership afforded by him and his followers in the revival of religious life (is acknowledged by all). The rise of the New England theology which constituted a revival of religious thought and acted as a doctrinal basis for the new style of preaching (was also a notable factor)." The leaders at this time, down to the beginning of the nineteenth century, were Jonathan Edwards, Joseph Bellamy, Samuel Hopkins, Stephen West, Jonathan Edwards the Younger, Nathaniel Emmons, and Timothy Dwight, and *all of these men were revivalists*. Most of them conducted theological schools in their own homes, and "the revival movement under the leadership of these men was directly responsible for a great increase in the membership of the church and in the number of young men devoting themselves to the ministry and for the expansion of religious work in general."

So, likewise, at Andover, of whom its historian says, "As the fading twilight of the eighteenth century brightened into the dawn of the nineteenth, a great wave of spiritual life, of religious and theological thought, and of missionary effort broke upon New England. The great awakening of the middle of the eighteenth century, to which a dramatic but disturbing element was added by the powerful preaching of Whitefield, had been followed, not unnaturally, by a corresponding reaction. The prolonged and exhausting war for our national independence, absorbing the thought and draining the resources of the people, was accompanied by a religious lethargy which was deepened, perhaps, by the scepticism and infidelity which marked the uprising of the French people with whom, on national grounds, Americans cherished a warm sympathy. But as the century was waning to its close, a little more than a hundred years ago, a religious revival as welcome as it was unexpected, stirred church and community in the little town of Yarmouth in this state. It was like the first faint flush in the eastern sky heralding the coming day; and like the morning light, it spread, noiselessly but surely. Not only New England but the Middle States and what was then the West, felt the spirit of the revival, and responded to its renewing life. It infused fresh vigor into the churches; it changed the face of society; it developed new methods of Christian effort and broadened the field of religious activity, and by quickening everywhere the evangelical spirit."

Many of the leading theologians of those great early schools participated again and again in revival meetings. Dr. Ezra Pond, professor at Bangor Theological Seminary for twenty years, preached with great power in a revival meeting in Brunswick, Maine, at which time large numbers were added to the church, including Governor R. P. Dunlap. This revival, says the historian of Bangor Seminary, "constituted an epoch in the history of the church in Brunswick. Previously it had been comparatively small, with a membership almost entirely of women. A prominent citizen, more witty than godly, said that the church was more scriptural; for while the Bible said 'seven women shall take hold of one man,' he had counted the people as they came from a morning prayer-meeting, and found eleven women to one man. But from the time of that revival, the church in Brunswick has ranked among the strong churches of the State. The revival also extended to the college, and among the students who then avowed themselves disciples of Christ was Henry B. Smith. This revival in college, and that of 1830, constituted an epoch in its religious history. President Appleton recorded his thankfulness that one student who was a church member had entered the college. The majority of the class of 1833, for the first time in the history of the college, were professors of religion."

In the middle of the nineteenth century, as everyone knows, the dominating influence in Oberlin College for thirty years was the greatest revivalist between Wesley and Moody, Charles G. Finney. Two educators, already located at Oberlin, Stanton and Whipple, wrote a letter to Finney dated January 10, 1835, urging Finney to come to Oberlin to head the school, in which they made this remarkable statement, " 'The harvest of the great valley is rotting and perishing for lack of *laboring men*. The spiritual death in our churches is alarming. The impenitent West is rushing to death, unresisted and almost unwarned. The whole Valley is over-run with antinomianism, Campbelliteism, Universalism and Infidelity—while Catholicism is fast taking possession of all our strongholds and is insidiously worming itself into the confidence of the people, and undermining the very foundations of pure religion. And the orthodox are quarreling among themselves.' They saw only one solution: there must be a great revival, such a revival as could be produced only by 'a new race of ministers' educated at a seminary 'established on high moral ground, . . . and decided in its revival spirit' and its support of the 'great and glorious reforms.' No such seminary, they felt, existed at that time in the West." . . . "Our eyes," continued Stanton and Whipple, "have for a long time been turned toward you, as possessing peculiar qualifications to fill a professorship in such an institution. Holding and teaching sentiments which we believe are in accordance with the Bible, and having been called by God to participate more largely in the revivals of the last nine years than any other man in the church, we could not but fix our attention on you as one whom God had designated for such a work . . . Recognizing these truths, and having full confidence in your qualifications, we strongly desire to become your pupils. . . . We cannot but think that the Providence of God directly calls upon you to become the professor of theology in that institution (Oberlin). If you should go there, nearly or quite all the theological students who left Lane, would place themselves at once under your instructions."

Supporting this thesis is the fact that the greatest evangelist of the nineteenth century, Dwight L. Moody, no educated man himself, felt it not contradictory to his divine calling as an evangelist to found a school for the training of men and women in a knowledge of the Word of God, the Moody Bible Institute, which remains a monument to his vision, and from which thousands of men and women, faithful to Christ and His Word, have gone out to preach the Gospel that Moody loved. Now in our generation another evangelist, with much more education than Moody was privileged to enjoy, has been led by the same Lord to be the moving agent in the founding of a new theological seminary, on the Pacific Coast.

Just when Dr. Fuller first conceived the idea of the establishment of a school for training young men for the Gospel ministry, cannot now be exactly determined. He allowed the idea to mature in his mind for some few years before he spoke to anyone about it. Dr. Fuller's wide knowledge of the apostasy setting in in the Christian Church, carrying multitudes of ministers away from the Gospel, undoubtedly gave him some conception of the enormous responsibility which is involved in the establishing of any such institution. Something of what that responsibility is, was expressed in a profound way, now nearly a hundred and forty years ago, at the founding of one of our most distinguished seminaries, Princeton, at the inauguration of which, August 12, 1812, Dr. Samuel Miller said, "When I cast an eye down the ages of eternity and think how important is the salvation of a single soul; when I realize how important is the office of a minister of the gospel who may be the happy instrument of saving many hundreds or thousands of souls; and when I remember how many and how momentous are the relations which a seminary intended solely for training up ministers bears to all the interests of men in the life that now is and especially in that which is to come; I feel as if the task of conducting such a seminary had an offense of responsibility connected with it which is enough to make us tremble."

As often happens with Christians in attempting to proceed in some great venture to which God has called, there was an initial mis-carriage. Early in 1946 Dr. Fuller issued a prospectus for what was to be known as the Fuller College of Missions and Evangelism, scheduled for opening September 24, 1946. The dean secured for this new school was Dr. William Evans, Ph.D., Litt.D., one of the great Bible teachers of America, and for many years Director of the Educational Department of the Moody Bible Institute. Among others secured for the faculty were the well-known missionary-authors, Dr. Robert Hall Glover, and Dr. Samuel M. Zwemer, recently of Princeton Theological Seminary. A prospectus was drawn up and a schedule of courses was settled upon. No building had been secured, and students, who were to be limited to one hundred for the opening year, would for the most part have to find living accommodations for themselves. For many reasons, some known, some that will never be known, probably, except that it was thus clearly the Lord's will, the entire project was dropped before the school was to have opened in the Fall of 1946. There are times when undertaking some task with enthusiasm we soon come to recognize, by various tokens sent to us of the Lord, that we are on the wrong road: so it was with the Fuller College of Missions and Evangelism. A generous financial arrangement was made with those who had given their time to the drawing up of courses, and all parted the best of friends, agreeing that the will of God must be done.

In the winter of 1946 Dr. Fuller invited Dr. Harold John Ockenga, of the Park Street Church, Boston, to come out to California to look over the entire field in the southern part of the State, and to canvass the possibility of the establishing of a theological school for the training of ministers where they might be thoroughly equipped in the fields of Bible, apologetics, theology, linguistics, evangelism, and all the major areas of a sound theological curriculum. At that time a large city lot had been purchased by Dr. Fuller, in open bidding, on which he told Dr. Ockenga that he with the funds of the Fuller Evangelistic Foundation would erect a building suitable for housing such an institution. Harold John Ockenga, after graduating from Taylor University and Westminster Theological Seminary, having been a student previously for two years at Princeton Theological Seminary, received the degree of Doctor of Philosophy for work in the field of European history from the University of Pittsburgh in 1934. In 1936 he began his brilliant pastorate at Park Street Church (Congregational), Boston, probably the most famous single church for the preaching of the Gospel in the history of New England. This is the church in which Lyman Beecher preached for years, A. Z. Conrad, and other notable men. Dr. Ockenga's ministry there has been greatly blessed of the Lord. His great church is filled morning and evening, with a prayer meeting often enjoying an attendance of over five hundred, and with a missionary budget now well over $110,000 a year. Dr. Ockenga is recognized as a scholar, preacher, orator, and a leader among men. He was so impressed with Dr. Fuller's desire for such a seminary, and the opportunity which Southern California offered for such an institution, that he agreed to undertake the gathering together of a faculty. It was to be a theological seminary receiving only students that had been graduated from accredited collegiate institutions, a seminary that would work immediately for accreditation, and be recognized as on a scholastic level with the best theological seminaries in North America. The first approach was made to Dr. Wilbur M. Smith, who was just closing his tenth year as a member of the faculty of the Moody Bible Institute, previously a Presbyterian pastor for some years, and since 1935 the editor of Peloubet's Select Notes on the International Sunday School Lessons. Dr. Fuller mentioned the matter to Dr. Smith in the Fall of 1946, and it would seem that probably one matter entered into in this correspondence deserves a place in this sketch of the early history of the seminary. Dr. Smith asked this question: "When it is launched, will there be a Board of Directors, or will it be a one-man institution; that is, will those who work there have something to say about the school and its administration, and especially its teaching functions; or will everything be determined by one man, which while you live would be yourself?" I wish it were possible to print every word of Dr. Fuller's long letter in reply, but that is not necessary in such a sketch as this. His answer to this particular question was as follows: "In the school the workers certainly would have something to say about the administration and teaching functions. In fact, if God should lead you to come to help me I should practically take my hands off as to choice of a faculty and curriculum. I know that you are of like mind and vision. I know my limitations." The one to whom he wrote this letter, who happens to be writing this book, would like to say at the close now of our first two years that Dr. Fuller has more than kept his word in this matter. No faculty of any graduate institution in America was ever given more liberty, genuine freedom, and absolute confidence in the molding of the curriculum and policies of a school than the members of the faculty of the Fuller Theological Seminary. More of this later. Dr. Ockenga began at once to approach certain other men in this country, seeking to discover whether they would be interested in joining such an enterprise if it were launched. The response he met was unquestionably another token of the leading of God.

On March 15, 1947, three of us gathered together in a

meeting in a private room at the Union League Club, Chicago. Dr. Fuller flew in from Pasedena, Dr. Ockenga came in from Boston, and Dr. Smith was living in the city at that time. After some hours of discussion, plans for securing members of the faculty were decided upon, and it was agreed that a second meeting should be held six weeks later. That meeting lasted for two days, and was held in the offices of the Taylor Foundation in the Civic Opera Building, Chicago. On the first day we were joined by Dr. Carl F. H. Henry, who, in the meantime, had shown great interest in the founding of the seminary. Dr. Henry, after graduating from Wheaton College and the Northern Baptist Theological Seminary, Chicago, where he received a Doctor of Theology degree, had been for six years Associate Professor of Theology, then Professor of Theology and Philosophy, and then Chairman of the Department of Theology and Philosophy of Religion at the Northern Baptist Theological Seminary, one of the most important conservative theological schools in North America. He had also been Visiting Professor at Wheaton College and at the Gordon College of Theology and Missions in Boston. To anticipate for a moment, Dr. Henry in the summer of 1949 received the Doctor of Philosophy degree from Boston University. He is the author of a number of outstanding books, including *Remaking the Modern Mind*, volumes that have created extensive discussion, have been enthusiastically reviewed in our best theological journals, and are often found quoted in the more important contemporary theological literature of our country.

On the second day we were joined by two other men who were to become members of the faculty. One was Dr. Everett F. Harrison, graduate of the University of Washington, with a master's degree from Princeton University, graduate of Princeton Theological Seminary, with a doctorate degree from Dallas Theological Seminary, and today a candidate for a Doctor of Philosophy degree in the University of Pennsylvania; Professor of Semitics and Old Testament Literature, 1928–1930 and 1932–1935, and Professor of New Testament Literature and Exegesis, 1935–1940, 1944–1947, in the Dallas Theological Seminary of Dallas, Texas. The other was Dr. Harold Lindsell, graduate of Wheaton College, with a doctorate degree in history, from New York University in Education, with graduate study in the College of the City of New York and Harvard University; Professor for three years in Columbia Bible College, and Professor of Missions and Associate Professor of Church History, 1944–1947, and Chairman of the Division of History and Science, 1945–1947, in the Northern Baptist Theological Seminary of Chicago. That meeting lasted from eight in the morning until five o'clock in the afternoon.

The author of this book will never forget that day. Dr. Ockenga came with a huge folder of correspondence and data, and perfectly arranged agenda of subjects for discussion. The meeting opened with a prolonged period of prayer, in which every person present participated. There seemed to be in those hours an unusual consciousness of the presence of God, giving wisdom, liberty in discussion, prompting suggestions, keeping us from disastrous mistakes, and, hour by hour, knitting us together in a fellowship which we knew was rare upon earth, even in Christian educational institutions. No restriction seemed to rest upon anyone. Everything was placed out in the open on the table. There was no other board to consult, no outside body of men from which approval or disapproval had to be sought. We were not drawing up suggestions for someone else to carry out, or to disapprove. We knew that day we were laying a foundation, and a recognition of a responsibility placed upon us of God, a deep, constant desire to know and follow only His perfect will rested upon us.

It had been generally understood in the correspondence of the preceding two months that it would hardly be possible to open the doors of a new theological seminary any

FULLER THEOLOGICAL SEMINARY 189

earlier than the Fall of 1948. Dr. Henry and Dr. Smith had had a long previous meeting together in Chicago and had sent Dr. Fuller a telegram, a part of which read: "We cannot announce plan without good advertising literature and catalogue. This could not be available until July. Moreover we need assurance of one more professor and registrar before advertising can be written. Ten months of preparation and wide publicity in press not a wasted year. None of us will ever let you down. We all believe this is our life-work. Great things are before us." In reply to this telegram Dr. Fuller sent us a wire reading: "God has worked so marvelously we should do our very best. Do not favor seventeen months' delay unless He absolutely closes doors." I believe it was our common feeling as we began our discussion on that momentous day that we could hardly expect that our seminary could begin to really function with an adequate studentbody before the Fall of 1948. But about the middle of the day the question came up for final decision, and within two hours of quiet, calm discussion we were all agreed that we would, with the help of God, announce the opening of the seminary *that Fall*. Thus only four months were left between that day when the seminary took its initial form, and the day the new school would open its doors to students, if God should send them. Dr. Henry prepared some very attractive advertising material, a copy of which was sent to the more important conservative weekly and monthly periodicals in our country. (*Christian Century* refused the opening advertisement, and has never been offered another.) Applications began to flow in at once—another token indeed of God's clear leading. When school opened, October 1, forty-seven men, graduates of colleges and universities in this country, including Dartmouth, Princeton, Harvard, Wheaton, the University of California, the University of Minnesota, etc., were registered. Four were registered who had already had one year of work at Princeton Theological

Seminary. One is almost safe in saying that no interdenominational (and rarely a denominational) theological seminary ever opened its first year with forty-seven students entering the Junior class. The faculty for that year and their respective positions were: Dr. Harold Lindsell, Registrar and Professor of Missions; Dr. Everett F. Harrison, Professor of New Testament; Dr. Carl F. H. Henry, Professor of Theology and Philosophy; Dr. Wilbur M. Smith, Professor of Apologetics. Dr. Harold J. Ockenga served as President *in absentia*, being with us at the opening of the school, when he delivered the baccalaureate address, and returning for two weeks of ministry among the students early in 1948.

It is now necessary to go back a little on the calendar to the matter of property, which became critical just at the time decisions were being made regarding the opening of the school in 1947 or 1948. A beautiful estate on South Orange Grove Avenue, known as the Cravens Estate, with a magnificent brick building upon it of thirty-two rooms, lovely gardens, and ample space for growth, was about to be sold at auction. The building itself probably cost a million dollars; the value of the land must represent nearly a quarter of a million dollars. Among others who it was reported were going to bid for this was a group of rich men who intended to make it a social club. They could have bid any figure that was asked, and could outbid almost anyone. Initial bids were sent through the mail. The Fuller Foundation made an offer. The day came for the bids to be opened, and then the property was placed before the public for open bidding. Some bankers had been joking the day before about a man, Charles E. Fuller, and his lawyer, who had been saying that God answered prayer and that if it was His will the property would come to the Foundation. That morning the bids were opened. The bid of the Foundation was the highest of those received in the mail. The presiding judge simply said, "I have a bid here from the Fuller Evangelistic Foundation for

$145,000.00. Do I hear any other bid?" A dead silence came over the courtroom, which had been very noisy during preceding bidding on other properties. Not a word was uttered. Within two minutes the property came into the possession of the Fuller Foundation. An inquiry was made later as to why the broker for this group of rich men had not come down to bid. His answer was, "I do not know why I did not go down. The night before I had it on my mind that I must go and bid. I do not know why I did not go." This also seemed at the time a mark of God's direct leading. It gave us a building for our students, a place for faculty offices, and for the library, a room for a chapel and ample quarters for a dining room. Some months later it was recognized that the zoning of Pasadena for that part of South Orange Grove Avenue would not, unless it was changed, allow for a seminary to function on these grounds. This was a blow to all of us at the time, but God wonderfully opened new doors to take care of this unexpected shift of plans. The large educational building of the Lake Avenue Congregational Church for six days a week for all the weeks and months of the seminary session was arranged for, and classes and chapel are held there. Faculty members have small offices there, and the dining room is located there. Dr. Fuller was able subsequently to purchase the large Livingstone Hotel, where single students are now housed. Two other buildings amply provide for our married students. At the original property on Orange Grove, faculty members still have their private studies. God gave us this property, however, with which we could advertise our school and open with adequate accommodations. Every school has had its serious problems and often its disappointments. God knows best. Somehow no feeling of discouragement came to anyone in the seminary when a temporary change of quarters was found necessary.

Of the first year of the seminary no history need here be written. This is the life of Dr. Fuller, not the history of the seminary. The second year opened with notable additions to our faculty and with one hundred and ten students in attendance for the Junior and Middle years, all of them carrying college degrees, full assurance to all of us that the entire nation was recognizing the value of what Fuller Seminary was undertaking, the quality of its faculty, and the adequacy of its training. There came to us for the second year two additional members of the faculty and a librarian. Dr. Gleason Leonard Archer, Jr., graduate of Harvard University, receiving from the same institution a Doctor of Philosophy degree, a graduate also of Princeton Theological Seminary, for three years instructor in German and Latin, Suffolk University, Boston, and for four years the assistant pastor under Dr. Ockenga of Park Street Church, Boston, came as the Professor of Biblical Lauguages. It has been rumored that Dr. Archer took every course in Semitics offered in Harvard University, and has a control of sixteen languages. As Associate Professor of Apologetics Dr. Edward John Carnell joined the faculty, graduate of Wheaton College and of Westminster Theological Seminary, with a Doctor of Theology degree from Harvard University, and a Doctor of Philosophy degree from Boston University. He had been Associate Professor of Philosophy at Gordon College and Gordon Divinity School for four years before coming to the Fuller Seminary. His well-known work on apologetics was recognized at once as a major contribution to the subject. Dr. Arnold D. Ehlert, graduate of Dallas Theological Seminary, where he was Assistant Librarian for six years, carrying a Doctor of Theology degree from the same seminary, came to be our librarian.

In the fall of 1949, the Fuller Theological Seminary opened with 155 students, forming one of the largest conservative theological seminaries, undenominationally related, in the United States, and all within a period of two and one-half years. How good God has been to us, what a miracle He has worked for us here in Southern California. Three members of the faculty were added, as follows: Dr. Herbert S. Mekeel, Dean and Acting Professor of Practical Theology, graduate of the University of Michigan, student at McMaster University, The Biblical Seminary, and Union Theological Seminary, New York, Assistant in History in the University of Michigan for two years, the gifted pastor for the last fourteen years of the very influential First Presbyterian Church of Schenectady, New York, where he has had a great influence over young men. From his congregation alone over sixty young men have declared their intention of entering the ministry since his pastorate began there. Dr. William S. LaSor, graduate of the University of Pennsylvania and of Princeton Theological Seminary, with a Doctor of Philosophy degree from Dropsie College for Hebrew and Cognate Learning, who had been the Chairman of the Department of Religion in Lafayette College since 1946, a Presbyterian pastor for some years preceding that, came to be the Associate Professor of Old Testament. He also has control of sixteen languages, including nearly all of the Semitic field, in addition to Egyptian and Babylonian. As Professor of Biblical Theology we have Dr. Bela Vasady, for many years Professor of Religious Philosophy and Education, and for four years Professor of Religious Philosophy and Education in the Reform Theological Seminary, Papa, Hungary, for six years, 1928–1934, Professor of Reformed Dogmatic and Ethics in the Reformed Theological Seminary, Sarospatak, Hungary, for six years Professor of Reformed Dogmatics in the Divinity Faculty of the University (1934–39) and President of the Theological Department of the Reformed College, 1943–49, at Debrecen, Hungary, and Guest Professor of Theology at Princeton Theological Seminary, 1947–49. In addition to these, we have other men from the outside giving courses in Christian life, public speech, etc.

The student body is one which the faculty believes is quite unusual, at least we are continually grateful for the men God has sent to us. All of them, as far as we know, have had a definite experience of regeneration. Many have been through the war, and are, as all returning veterans are in school, characterized by unchanging seriousness. Some of them entered their respective universities and colleges to study mechanical engineering, electrical engineering, chemistry, physics, or some of the other sciences, and then toward the end of their senior year, or soon afterwards, or even during the war, were divinely called of God to enter into the Christian ministry. Many of our students, possibly forty per cent, will become missionaries, others pastors, some teachers, workers among Inter-Varsity groups, some assistant pastors: every one of them is looking forward to a full lifetime of work in some Christian service. While the studies, as in any true seminary, are difficult, and require real intellectual exertion, yet we have had very, very few who could not make a passing grade, which grading, by the way, is called "stiff." Most of our men have done thorough work, and a few are doing brilliant work, as in every other school. Probably it is not necessary to mention this, but while we have no rules in reference to these matters, there is no smoking anywhere among our students, either in private or publicly, and of course there is no drinking anywhere in the seminary, either on the part of students or faculty upon any occasion whatever.

The library of Fuller Theological Seminary may already be said to be a rather important collection. It contains something over 15,000 volumes, many of which are quite rare. Just as the seminary was being founded, two book dealers in this country brought from the British Isles some great collections of material, and they allowed one of the members of the faculty to have first choice in all these treasures, so that many of the great standard works in theology, Biblical interpretation, the history of doctrine, Christology, etc., are already in our possession, in addition, of course, to the essential tools for efficient library work. In 1948, we were privileged to purchase the theological section of the famous Fyens Stiftsbibliothek of Odense, Denmark. This collection of 3,000 volumes was originally part of the larger Fyens collection of some 30,000 volumes. Most of the books are from the 18th and 19th centuries with some from the 17th and a few from the 16th. A great many are in full leather or half-leather bindings or vellum. German and Latin predominate with some in French and other languages. It is our conviction that many of these titles will turn out to be the only copies on the American continent. The dealer in Copenhagen, from whom the purchase was made, said of the collection, "In the one-hundred-year-old history of our firm, we have never had such a beautiful collection of the theology of the 18th century."

This year, 1949, we have acquired another very important collection, first seen by Dr. Ockenga, in London, in the preceding summer, a collection of over 900 volumes of Catholic and anti-Catholic writings, which had been gathered together over nearly a century by the National Club of London. Many of these volumes are not to be found in any other library of America. Some of the quartos and folios, in Latin, are the basic works for all historical studies in the development of the Catholic Church in Europe.

In addition to the books belonging to the Fuller Seminary proper, Dr. Smith's private library of 14,000 volumes is accessible daily to all students, and each professor, of course, has his own extensive library, available to those doing research in particular areas. Probably, all together, the seminary and its faculty make available to the student body a collection of not much less than 35,000 volumes. The library subscribes to over 150 serials, including practically all the important theological, archaeological and biblical quarterlies, published in Europe and North America. The library has initiated a *Bulletin,* apparently the only publication of its kind being issued at this time by the library of any theological seminary in North America, an undertaking that has had strong commendation of theological librarians throughout the country.

A beautiful administration building for Fuller Theological Seminary has been planned, and funds are now being gathered together for its erection, a picture of which proposed structure will be found toward the end of this volume. On the first floor will be the administrative offices for Dr. Fuller, the President, the Dean, Registrar, Bursar, Business Manager, the Board of Regents, and their complementary secretarial offices, also a large social hall—in addition to the lounge and game room of the basement—and a seminar room, separated by sound-proof partitions. The entire area of the second floor will be devoted to a beautifully designed chapel, seating approximately 250 persons, the library, and a large classroom seating 150 students. The main reading room of the library will contain approximately 2700 square feet of floor space, and will comfortably seat in excess of one hundred students. The library stack room is designed to accommodate a library of 100,000 volumes. On the third floor will be located offices for the professors, classrooms, and the professors' lounge. The fourth floor will be given over to classrooms and a seminar room. The building has been designed in the traditional style of modified Gothic, and will be as commodious a seminary structure as is to be found anywhere west of the North Atlantic states.

A word should possibly be said about the literary productivity of the faculty. Many of the professors are already well known for books they have written. Seven volumes have been published just this year by our faculty members, and many others are in process of composition. A new series has just been undertaken to be known as the Fuller Theological Seminary Bibliographical Studies, under the general editorship of three members of the faculty. The first one is now about to be issued as I am writing this chapter, a seventy-page volume, *A Basic Semitic Bibliography*, with extensive annotations, by Dr. William S. LaSor.

Recently a group of a large Protestant denomination in this country, always emphasizing the very best educational equipment for its ministers, sent a committee to investigate Fuller Seminary to see if this group could accept graduates of our seminary when they came up for ordination. A few lines from this report might well be placed in this chapter:

"Fuller Theological Seminary is a strong and going institution, with every indication of permanence. This is not an ephemeral or temporary institution.

"The scholastic standards are high, on a par with any seminary in the country. The B.A. degree or its equivalent is required for entrance. Two years of Hebrew and three of Greek are required for graduation. The class room work is of a high order. The seminary is too new to be accredited by the American Association of Theological Schools, but such accreditation has been applied for, and there seems no reason why it should not be granted, at the proper time.

"The theological point of view is Calvinistic, and completely within the Reformed tradition.

"We were impressed by the spirit and the attitude of the student body. They are in earnest, they are consecrated, and they are thoroughly evangelistic, and there did not seem to be any undue preponderance of fanatics. There was a great deal of quiet humor. We were convinced that there was a genuine appreciation and understanding of the spirit of Christian love and Christian tolerance.

"Your committee is aware of the fact that Fuller Seminary has been described as 'divisive' by respected leaders of the Church in general. As far as we understand what is meant by this term, we do not find its use justified. We would contrast it with other seminaries and Bible schools, denominational and undenominational, whose graduates seem to feel that they are called upon to save the Church from heretical preaching or teaching, or that their chief mission is to attack the opinions of their brother ministers. We did not find any traces of this attitude among either the members of the faculty or students with whom we talked."

Without going into detail concerning other features of seminary life, the following statement should be made: Fuller Theological Seminary presently offers only the degree of Bachelor of Divinity, the granting of which must be preceded by the attainment of a standard bachelor's degree on the collegiate level. The Bachelor of Divinity degree is granted upon the completion of the standard three-year theological curriculum at this institution, or upon completion of at least one year of residence work (in the Senior year) at the Seminary with sufficient transferable credit from some other standard theological seminary or seminaries. The first class will be graduated in May, 1950, after which time it is anticipated that graduate work will be offered leading to higher theological degrees.

We might ask now, How was it possible for a seminary with such standards to gather within sixteen months of its initial announcement one hundred and fifty-five university and college graduates, at the extreme southwestern end of the United States, and such a faculty as has here been named, each of them coming to Fuller Seminary from important and influential positions in the Christian field? Humanly speaking, confidence in two persons is responsible for this: first, confidence in the character and purpose and ministry of Dr. Charles E. Fuller, and secondly, confidence in the integrity of the ideals and the leadership of Dr. Harold J. Ockenga. Dr. Fuller now sees unfolding before him a far greater institution than he ever dreamed of when he first began to sketch a prospectus for a school of evangelism. God terminated the plans for one before they even began to be carried into execution that Dr. Fuller's mind might be open and free for God's plan for an even greater school. The spirit of evangelism which has so bountifully rested upon the thought and ministry of our founder abides upon the faculty and student body. It has been founded for training gifted men to know, interpret, and preach the Word of God, and this means, all of us are confident, that out of this student body will come a glorious group of men to be evangelists, missionaries, pastors, and teachers, and perhaps, if God wills, but this is wholly in God's keeping, a prophet for such a day as this.

There are, however, explanations much greater than all human factors accounting for the sudden rise and the healthy condition of our school, and that is nothing else than the leading of the Spirit of God. He gave Dr. Fuller the original vision, and at the same time laid this burden upon the heart of Dr. Ockenga. He then prepared the hearts of these members of the faculty, some the first year, some the second, and some this third year, loosening the ties which had bound them affectionately to their former institutions, and enabling them to cast their lot with the new seminary on the Pacific Coast. Then, of course, there has been the individual leading of God in the hearts of these young men. A few, of course, came who left the first year, two or three the second year, and there will probably be some leaving this year; every seminary has this experience, but no one is to be found in the student body or faculty today, as far as known, who does not have a deep conviction in his heart that thus far the Lord has led him to the seminary in Pasadena. A passion for study, a confidence in the Word of God, precious fellowship in prayer, a longing to be wholly yielded to the Spirit of God, a vision of preaching the gospel to the whole world, a deep interest in every evangelistic movement, are all to be observed in the daily life of the school, for which we give God unceasing praise.

CHAPTER XIV

A RECENT PROGRAMME OF THE
OLD FASHIONED REVIVAL HOUR

On Sunday afternoon, September 11, having been away from home for some weeks, I eagerly turned on my radio at four o'clock to hear a rebroadcast of the Old Fashioned Revival Hour for the preceding week, Labor Day Sunday, September 4. I had not listened to the opening musical program for more than five minutes when I felt convinced that, whatever the message might be, this was one of the finest musical programs the Old Fashioned Revival Hour had enjoyed for a long time, though all of its music is usually far above the average. As the minutes passed, I felt persuaded that this was the program which would form an excellent chapter in our book. Of course, there had been no hint of this on my part to Dr. Fuller, the choir, or the quartet. Dr. Fuller told me later, upon my inquiry, that there were forty-two hundred people in the Municipal Auditorium at Long Beach for this program. I think one may safely say that there is no man in America today who at his regularly scheduled Sunday service preached to forty-two hundred people on Labor Day Sunday, whether in the morning, afternoon, or evening. The gracious approval of God, after all these many years of the simple preaching of the gospel, could not be more emphatically displayed than in this great gathering of people to hear a program which has been on the air now for so many years. Without further comment, I would like to set forth the various numbers of this program as they appeared, with-

The Proposed Main Building for the Fuller Theological Seminary

THE OLD FASHIONED REVIVAL HOUR

out any announcement on the part of Dr. Fuller, and then give, in full, the gospel message which was delivered that afternoon.

The hour opened with the choir singing, as I have seldom heard them sing, "There's a New Name Written Down in Glory," the chorus of which reads as follows:

> "There's a new name written down in glory
> And it's mine, O yes, it's mine!
> And the white robed angels sing the story,
> 'A sinner has come home.'
> For there's a new name written down in glory,
> And it's mine, O yes, it's mine!
> With my sins forgiven I am bound for heaven,
> Never more to roam."

DR. FULLER: "All right, let's stand and sing 'Heavenly Sunshine' to all those who are in radio land." (As usual, these thousands of people shook hands one with the other, and then "Heavenly Sunshine" was sung the second time.)

QUARTET: "Will Jesus Find us Watching," by Fanny J. Crosby.

> "When Jesus comes to reward His servants,
> Whether it be noon or night,
> Faithful to Him, will he find us watching
> With our lamps all trimmed and bright?
>
> Blessed are those whom the Lord finds watching,
> In His glory they shall share;
> If He shall come at the dawn or midnight,
> Will He find us watching there?
>
> Chorus:
> O can we say we are ready, brother,
> Ready for the soul's bright home?
> Say, will He find you and me still watching,
> Waiting, waiting, when the Lord shall come?"

Dr. Fuller extends a welcome to the audience, and invites those living in or visiting Southern California to attend the broadcast on subsequent Sundays, commenting on the fact that during the last few weeks ministers and missionaries from Canada, India, China, South and Central America had made themselves known in his audience, which, he added, had been a wonderful encouragement to him.

CHOIR: "I Surrender All."

> "All to Jesus I surrender,
> All to Him I freely give
> I will ever love and trust Him,
> In His presence daily live.
>
> All to Jesus I surrender
> Humbly at His feet I bow,
> Worldly pleasures all forsaken,
> Take me, Jesus, take me now.
>
> All to Jesus I surrender,
> Make me, Saviour, wholly Thine;
> Let me feel the Holy Spirit—
> Truly know that Thou art mine.
>
> Chorus:
> I surrender all, I surrender all,
> All to Thee, my blessed Saviour,
> I surrender all."

Dr. Fuller mentions the "Heart-to-Heart-Talks," including "Outlines of Prophecy," which are issued every month and sent free to all those who write and ask for them. He speaks especially to those who are listening to the Old Fashioned Revival Hour for the first time, and gives the famous mailing address: Charles E. Fuller, Post Office Box 123, Los Angeles, California.

QUARTET: "The Old Account Was Settled Long Ago," by F. W. Graham.
(I think this song was new to me, though it is really old, and it brought a great blessing to my own heart.)

"There was a time on earth, when in the book of heav'n
An old account was standing for sins yet unforgiv'n;
My name was at the top, and many things below,
I went unto the keeper, and settled long ago.

O sinner, seek the Lord, repent of all your sin,
For thus He has commanded, if you would enter in
And then if you should live a hundred years below,
Up there you'll not regret it, you settled long ago.

Chorus:
Long ago, long ago
Yes, the old account was settled long ago
And the record's clear today,
For He washed my sins away
When the old account was settled long ago."

CHOIR: "When I Kneel Down to Pray"

"Somehow the Saviour seems a little nearer,
When I kneel down to pray,
And fellowship with him a little nearer,
When I kneel down to pray."

Chorus:
"I know that He will always hear me,
For He is never far away;
And yet He seems a little close to me,
When I kneel down to pray."

Mrs. Fuller reads from the letters. (An entire chapter is given to this part of the Old Fashioned Revival Hour, and for this reason the text of the letters read on this particular occasion is here omitted.)

The audience with the choir sings, "I Love to Tell the Story," the first stanza of which is:

> "I love to tell the story, of unseen things above,
> Of Jesus and His glory, of Jesus and His love.
> I love to tell the story, because I know 'tis true,
> It satisfies my longings, as nothing else can do.
>
> Chorus:
> I love to tell the story! 'T will be my theme in glory
> To tell the old, old story of Jesus and His love."

A brief, earnest prayer by Mr. Daniel P. Fuller, Dr. Fuller's only son, closing with the words, "that in these closing days there might be a sweeping revival that will bring many into Thy kingdom."

CHOIR: "Some Day He'll Make It Plain."

(This is the one hymn sung that afternoon so well known to everyone that we do not think it is necessary to repeat it here.)

QUARTET: "How Can I Help but Love Him?" (Between the first and second stanzas, Mr. Rudy Atwood plays this glorious gospel song through on the piano with his remarkable variations.)

> "Down from His splendor in glory He came,
> Into a world of woe;
> Took on Himself all my guilt and my shame,
> Why should He love me so?
>
> I am unworthy to take of His grace,
> Wonderful grace so free;
> Yet Jesus suffered and died in my place,
> E'en for a soul like me.
>
> Chorus:
> How can I help but love Him
> When He loved me so?
> How can I help but love Him,
> When He loved me so?"

Dr. Fuller gives his regular announcement, "You are listening to the Old Fashioned Revival Hour," etc.

CHOIR: "Some Bright Morning." (This was sung with great liveliness, and must have brought blessing to multitudes.)

> "Be not a-weary, for labor will cease,
> Some glad morning;
> Turmoil will change into infinite peace,
> Some bright morning.
>
> Labor well done shall receive its reward,
> Some glad morning;
> Thou who art faithful shall be with the Lord,
> Some bright morning.
>
> Chorus:
> Some bright morning, some glad morning,
> When the sun is shining in th' eternal sky;
> Some bright morning, some glad morning . . .
> We shall see the Lord of Harvest by and by."

QUARTET: "Good Night and Good Morning."

> "When comes to the weary a blessed release,
> When upward we pass to His kingdom of peace,
> When free from the woes that on earth we must bear,
> We'll say, 'good-night' here, but 'good-morning' up there.
>
> When home-lights we see shining brightly above,
> Where we shall be soon, thro' His wonderful love,
> We'll praise Him who called us His heaven to share,
> We'll say 'good-night' here, but 'good-morning' up there.
>
> Chorus:
> Good morning up there where Christ is the Light,
> Good morning up there where cometh no night;
> When we step from this earth to God's heaven so fair,
> We'll say 'good-night' here, but 'good-morning' up there."

Dr. Fuller begins his message by reading aloud the text, Exodus 12:12,13.

"Has your heart been greatly rejoiced and refreshed by these wonderful songs? I know it has. I have been lifted up. How thankful we ought to be that we can make melody in our heart, and sing with our lips the great themes of redemption and faith.

"There are three portions of the Word of God I would like to read to you in connection with this very important subject, Christ our Passover. May I stop and say, pray with me now that many souls may find Christ. We are not putting on this broadcast for any show, but we are putting it on to beseech men and women everywhere to be reconciled to Jesus Christ. 'For I will go through the land of Egypt in that night, and will smite all the first-born in the land of Egypt, both man and beast: and against all the gods of Egypt, I will execute judgments: I am Jehovah. And the blood shall be to you for a token upon the houses where ye are: and when I see the blood, I will pass over you, and there shall no plague be upon you to destroy you, when I smite the land of Egypt' (Exodus 12:12,13). 'By faith he forsook Egypt, not fearing the wrath of the king: for he endured as seeing him who is invisible' (Hebrews 11:28). 'Purge out the old leaven, that ye may be a new lump, even as ye are unleavened. For our passover also hath been sacrificed, even Christ' (I Corinthians 5:7).

"Last Lord's Day we gave you the setting, or the occasion for Moses' instituting the Passover; that is, the tenth and last judgment was about to come down upon Egypt, the death of the first-born was about to take place, and in this critical hour God speaks unto Moses (in the 12th chapter of Exodus) and gives him, first of all, the plan of redemption, the purpose of this plan of redemption, and the penalty attached to those who refused to accept the plan of redemption. Furthermore, this 12th chapter of Exodus sets forth one of the clearest types of Calvary to be found anywhere in the entire

Bible. In this Passover scene the Old and New Testaments are beautifully linked together, beautifully interwoven. Exodus 12 sets forth the instituting of the Passover, pointing to Christ our sacrifice, as mentioned in I Corinthians 5:7. Now follow with me God's plan of redemption as set forth in this chapter.

"God here reveals the way out, that is, the plan of redemption whereby His people will be saved from physical death. This plan of redemption is an exact type of the plan which God has revealed in the cross of Christ; that is, all who will hear, and act upon what they hear regarding God's plan of deliverance from Satan, sin, and the coming lake of fire, will be saved from spiritual death, that is, eternal separation from God. You *hear* God is not willing that any should perish. You *hear* that Christ died for you. But let me ask, how do you individually act upon that which you hear? Do you *really* believe, that is, personally appropriate what God has done for you? If you hear with an open ear and obedient heart, you will be redeemed, become a new creation, and will manifest your redemption by your works of righteousness, that you really have passed from death unto life, for faith without works is dead.

"Now here is the *plan* as revealed in the 12th chapter of Exodus. Take your Bibles and let us go back to verse 3, and search the Scriptures, for after all is said and done, heaven and earth will pass away, but God's Word will never pass away. You notice in verse 3 we have the time set: 'Speak ye unto all the congregation of Israel, saying, In the tenth day of this month they shall take to them every man a lamb, according to the house of their fathers, a lamb for an house.' 'They shall take to them every man a lamb.' No other animal will do. God does not mix up types and put in extraneous words. Verse 5 tells us the kind of lamb: 'Your lamb shall be without blemish, a male of the first year: ye shall take it out from the sheep, or from the goats. And ye shall keep it up until the fourteenth day of the same month.' Notice the wording: 'And the whole assembly of the congregation of Israel shall kill it in the evening.' Very specific. How this looks forward to the cross of Christ! Let us just see for a moment Christ our Passover. How beautifully this 14th chapter of Exodus foreshadows. Christ is spoken of as the Lamb of God which taketh away the sin of the world—John 1:29. I Peter 1:18,19 —'Forasmuch as ye know that ye were not redeemed with corruptible things, as silver and gold, from your vain conversation, received by tradition from your fathers; but with the precious blood of Christ, as of a lamb without blemish and without spot.' O how beautifully they dove-tail together. Taken out from the sheep—that is, Christ was made like unto His brethren of the household of faith. He took upon Himself the form of sinful flesh. He was taken out from among His brethren. Then note, please, 'the whole assembly of the congregation of Israel shall kill it in the evening.' Need I remind you, 'Ye men of Israel, hear these words; Jesus of Nazareth, a man approved of God among you by miracles and wonders and signs . . . him ye have taken and by wicked hands have crucified and slain' (Acts 2:22,23). Note, the lamb must be slain. The lamb's blood must be shed, that Israel might have life on that awful night. I go over to the New Testament, and I read these words: 'For God so loved the world that he gave His only begotten Son, that whosoever believeth in him should not perish, but have everlasting life.' I read again in I Peter 2:24, speaking of Christ: 'Who his own self bare our sins in his own body on the tree, that we, being dead to sins, should live unto righteousness: by whose stripes ye were healed.' It is not sufficient that the blood is shed, but that over each dwelling, each one willing to escape death, must apply the shed blood to his own door with a bunch of hyssop. 'And they shall take of the blood, and put it on the two side-posts, and on the lintel, upon the houses wherein they shall eat it . . . And ye shall take a bunch of hyssop, and dip it in the blood that is in the basin, and strike the lintel and the two side-posts with the blood that is in the basin; and none of you shall go out of the door of his house until the morning' (Exodus 12:7,22). I could preach for hours upon that. You and I are not going out of the house until the morning when Christ comes for His own. Note please—the blood must be on the outside of the door, so that everyone could see it and know they were trusting in the shed blood, and there is no safety except behind the blood-stained doors. So Christ must be openly and publicly confessed. If you believe in your heart that God has raised Him from the dead, and confess Him with the mouth as the Lord Jesus Christ, thou shalt be saved. A hyssop—what is it? A low, clinging, earthly vine. Even a child could reach down and gather a bunch of hyssop. It was within the reach of everyone—a lamb for his house, and the provision, right where they were, to reach down and with the bunch of hyssop, dip it in the basin of blood, and strike it on the door-post.

"Now let us consider the *purpose* of this plan of redemption. What did God send His Son into this world to die for sin for? Exodus 12:13,23—'And the blood shall be to you for a token upon the houses where ye are: and when I see the blood, I will pass over you, and there shall no plague be upon you to destroy you, when I smite the land of Egypt. . . . For Jehovah will pass through to smite the Egyptians; and when he seeth the blood upon the lintel, and on the two side-posts, Jehovah will pass over the door, and will not suffer the destroyer to come in unto your houses to smite you.' When the death angel came at midnight, he did not inquire into what kind of people lived within the house, whether they were old or young, whether they were rich or poor, whether they were old or young, whether they were members of any kind of special social organization or civic group. No! The death angel simply ascertained whether there was the applied shed blood of the slain lamb on the door, and if the shed blood was there, he passed over, he passed on, and those within were saved from death, not because of their works of righteousness, but because they were trusting in the blood that was shed. *Amen!* The blood on the door signified that the people within that house believed, accepted, God's plan of redemption from death, and were trusting God's word as follows: 'When I see the blood, I will pass over you.' It was the blood that saved the Israelites from physical death. It is the blood of Christ, and that alone, that saves us from spiritual death. The lamb did not save by its innocence, its spotlessness, its example, but by its shed blood. And how the prince of the power of the air, Satan, hates to have the blood of Christ preached over the radio! As by its death and shed blood they were saved, so it was not the innocence, spotlessness, or example of Christ which saved us, but His shed blood on the cross, His dying in our place and stead—Christ our Passover, slain for us.

"Now let us think of the *penalty*. Will you listen carefully? Believers, pray with me. The penalty attached to those who refuse to accept God's plan of redemption—thank God I am free from the blood of every man and woman in the sound of my voice today—'And it came to pass at midnight, that Jehovah smote all the firstborn in the land of Egypt, from the first-born of Pharaoh that sat on his throne unto the first-born of the captive that was in the dungeon; and all the first-born of cattle' (Exodus 12:29). In every home where the shed blood of the lamb was not found, the death angel went in, the first-born was slain, and when the death angel finished his work that night—listen—there was in every house either a dead lamb and the applied blood, or a dead child—no middle ground, no exceptions. God is no respecter of persons. 'It is appointed unto man once to die, and after that the judgment.' He said, 'I have appointed a day wherein men will be judged by Christ Jesus' (Acts 17: 31). 'He that hath the Son hath life, and he that hath not the Son hath not life.' The blood was all that God looked at then. It is all God looks at now. 'For he hath made peace through the blood of the cross.' Suppose some Israelite had said on that awful night, 'I do not see any need for slaying the lamb. I will fasten the lamb to my door, and imitate its meekness, and purity, and try to be spotless, without sin and blame'? The first-born in that house would have died. God's plan of redemption is based upon the shed blood of the Lord Jesus. And on that night those behind the blood-sprinkled doors were not sleeping, or drinking, or carousing, or entertaining themselves in a foolish manner, but were watching, waiting. 'Watch, therefore, and be ready, for in such an hour as ye think not, the Son of Man shall come to execute judgment.' Are you under the blood? If not, you are lost. If you are under the blood, and have appropriated the shed blood, your life will manifest the works of redemption.

"Let us bow our heads in prayer while the choir sings an invitation number, 'Just as I am without one plea, but that Thy blood was shed for me.' Pray as they sing. And friends of radioland, as we are bringing the Old Fashioned Revival Hour to a close, will you take God at His word and come? He says, 'Come, let us reason together.' Will you take God at His word? God bless you. Kneel right down in your room, or by your bed, wherever you may be, look up into the Father's face through Jesus Christ and say, 'God be merciful to me a sinner, and save me.' While heads are bowed in this fine audience at Long Beach, put your hand up just before we leave the air and say, 'Pray for me.' God bless you. God bless you. There is no middle ground."

When the broadcast hour terminates, the invitation is continued for a few moments, after which a brief altar service is held, where trained personal workers talk with each one who has come forward, pointing to them the Way of Life.

We cannot close this chapter without a word regarding the song that has been sung for years in every service of the Old Fashioned Revival Hour, and which literally millions have learned to sing around the world. In 1899 a song was published entitled "Heavenly Sunlight," the words of which, written by the Rev. H. J. Zelley, began as follows:

> "Walking in the sunlight, all of my journey,
> Over the mountains, thru the deep vale;
> Jesus has said, 'I'll never forsake thee,'
> Promise divine that never shall fail.
>
> *Chorus:*
> Heavenly sunlight, heavenly sunlight,
> Flooding my soul with glory divine;
> Hallelujah! I am rejoicing,
> Singing His praises, Jesus is mine."

In the autumn of 1941, Dr. and Mrs. Fuller were having luncheon at "Ye Olde Oyster House" in Boston with Mr. and Mrs. Cutler B. Whitwell, who at this time were representing the Old Fashioned Revival Hour in the East. The Whitwells happened to remark, in discussing the conferences they had been holding that summer, that particular blessing was being found in the singing of the old song, "Heavenly Sunlight," of which, I believe, Dr. Fuller at that time had never heard. Mr. and Mrs. Whitwell sang it for the Fullers in the booth where luncheon was being enjoyed. Dr. Fuller says, "Later as we were driving up the Maine coast the song kept ringing in my ears and heart, and because I did not remember all the words and even the tune was not quite clear in my memory, I made my own version and I call it 'Heavenly

Sunshine.' We hummed it for days and the song came to mean so much to me that I decided quite suddenly one night to sing it over the air. Much to my surprise I found others loved it as much as I did, so I think God must have given us this little song to cheer up on the way at a time of great need in the world's history." Dr. Fuller's lines, as everyone knows, read as follow:

> "Heavenly sunshine, heavenly sunshine,
> Flooding my soul with glory Divine—
> Heavenly sunshine, heavenly sunshine,
> Hallelujah! Jesus is mine!"

All of his listeners can remember times in the programs of the Old Fashioned Revival Hour when Dr. Fuller would remark, "The spirit moves me to sing 'Heavenly Sunshine,' " and then he would sing it as a solo, after which he would have the entire congregation sing it, and, as the custom is, everyone turns around and shakes hands with two or three near-by.

This song has been heard around the world. I remember someone telling me a year or two ago that once during the war a large naval craft drew up in a harbor in one of the Far East countries, and the personnel asked the natives there, through an interpreter, to sing something in their native language. A great crowd of children who had gathered down near the wharf started to sing "Heavenly Sunshine"!

Chapter XV

CHARLES E. FULLER THE MAN

In writing his second letter to the Corinthians, the Apostle Paul told the Christians at Corinth—whether to blame them or not we need not here debate—that which could be said of all men and women, some more, some less, an axiom for all human contact, "Ye look at the things that are before your face" (II Cor. 10:7, R.V.). In our final chapter concerning Dr. Fuller, let us look first at the things that are before our face, as one sees Dr. Fuller, and then we can watch him among people, in his home, and look for a moment, reverently, into his inner life, though no man can ever know fully the inner life of another, not even his own.

Dr. Fuller is what many Bible teachers and radio preachers are not, a strikingly handsome individual, wherever one sees him, on the street, in his office, on the platform, or in his home—a man six feet tall, weighing about two hundred and ten pounds, without a surplus ounce of flesh, with a healthy, ruddy glow in his strong face, hair that is almost white, brown eyes filled with the love of God and tenderness toward men, and a countenance lined with the marks that clearly tell of hard work, mastery of self, occupation with big things, and conflict with evil powers. I remember once speaking to Dr. Robert E. Speer after an evening service, accompanied by a Christian friend of mine. When we got outside of the building, my friend said to me, "His face is marked with the lines of a warrior who has fought valiantly for Christ." I am reminded of this when I look into the face of Dr. Fuller.

A Sunday Afternoon Audience in the Municipal Auditorium at Long Beach, listening to the Old Fashioned Revival Hour Programme

Although he dresses immaculately, he seems never to pay any attention to his clothes. He appears everywhere as a rugged, robust, energy-radiating man, who dresses not to draw attention to himself, but rather to give an impression of cleanliness, neatness, and refinement. I have never heard him mention anything he ever wore, with one exception—he has a great, broad-brimmed Texas hat, given to him by some friends when he was broadcasting once at Houston, of which he is very fond. It would appear ridiculous on some men; it is suited to him perfectly.

In all the many occasions I have been with Dr. Fuller, I have never heard him mention food once. I am sure he likes good, wholesome food, but he probably would rather have a bowl of corn meal mush at home than a steak dinner at a famous eating place. Apparently he is not an epicure, but, on the other hand, he is not aesthetic. I know some men who can tell you of big meals they have had in a hundred different places in America from early manhood down to their mature years. I do not think Dr. Fuller could recall the nature of any meal two days after he had eaten it. He likes comfort, but he can endure hardness, as he had to endure it for many years in his youth. He enjoys an atmosphere of refinement, but he is not fastidious. Dr. Fuller has a lovely home, but I am sure he could be happy, as he was for many of his earlier years, in a much simpler residence. Things as such apparently mean nothing to him, except he wants the best in anything that he purchases. He handles large sums of money, but he is not extravagant. He carefully watches expenditures, but he is noted for his generosity. Bills must be paid promptly, and he keeps a name of honor in every banking institution with which he carries on transactions. As far as I know, Dr. Fuller has no hobbies, strange to say. Though he spent years working in orange groves, I am sure he would hardly recognize a hoe or rake today, and would hesitate before picking one up for any work in the garden. He does not have a woodwork bench, nor does he work with tools. He is not a collector of books, coins, stamps, or antique furniture. It has been years since he played golf. While he enjoys, and once owned a speed boat, he does not have one today.

One thing everyone notices about the property Dr. Fuller possesses—everything must be kept up in excellent condition. I have even seen him brush dust off his car—because he likes everything spotlessly clean. His eagle eye would discover the slightest dent in any car he was driving, but he is not interested in the mechanics of an automobile, and does not spend time trying to improve an engine. I think the words which Paul wrote to Timothy in his last epistle apply to Dr. Fuller in a way in which they apply to few outstanding preachers of the gospel today: "No soldier on service entangleth himself in the affairs of this life; that he may please him who enrolled him as a soldier" (II Timothy 2:4). Dr. Fuller of necessity must give attention to many affairs, some of them of large proportions, but he is not entangled with them. He sits lightly to the things of this world.

Though he has spoken to crowds every week for years, probably the largest Sunday audience confronted by any preacher of the gospel, regularly, week after week, year after year, Dr. Fuller is himself a timid individual among strangers. He is at home on the platform when expounding the Word of God, but he is not at home standing in a crowd of people. On the other hand, he is not deliberately aloof. No seriously minded person is ever given the brush-off by Charles Fuller. He is ever courteous, always a gentleman, though it is not his nature to spend hours wrestling with the personal problems of some troubled Christian: some men have gifts in this direction who would not be able to do the work Dr. Fuller does. No Christian should be blamed for not having what some other Christian has, and

CHARLES E. FULLER THE MAN

none of us is to envy the talents of others. Dr. Fuller enjoys humor, but is rarely humorous. I have seen him laugh at Dr. Homer Hammontree's wonderful repertoire of stories for almost an hour at the dinner table, but I cannot recall hearing Dr. Fuller tell three stories in three years, though no doubt he has. He likes to talk to men, but dislikes small talk. As Mrs. Fuller one time remarked, "Charles cannot stand twittering, and . . . twitters, so I cannot have ——— in our home when Charles is there. It would drive him crazy."

And the mention of Mrs. Fuller leads straight to the paradise on this earth that he enjoys, namely, his home. In the official life of the great Joseph Parker of London, of another generation, we are told that when Mrs. Parker went into the city to shop, she would not tell her famous husband that she was going, for when he knew she was out of the house, he was paralyzed for work. Now I do not think Dr. Fuller is exactly paralyzed when Mrs. Fuller is away for a few hours, but they are seldom apart, and he only lives a full life when he is at home with his dear wife and his son. He is ever most gracious to the helpmeet God has given him. Thus in driving with them in a car, one does not hear the scolding, and the criticism, which has brought embarrassment to many who have ridden with those of whom one would never think such crudeness or discourtesy was possible. What home problems may arise are kept at home, not paraded before the public.

Moreover, in private Dr. Fuller is the same person he is in public. In such a home there is tenseness continually—not tension born of conflicts of personality, but the tension arising from great problems concerning this vast network of broadcasting, the purchase of property, the planning of long trips for speaking engagements, the tension that is created by doing great things, and knowing that the time is short, the kind of tension that makes people rise early in the morning and spend long, hard days at work, retiring early at night only for the sake of getting the rest that will permit another long day of work within a few hours.

One item cannot be passed by in this chapter, and that is Snooky, the little black cocker spaniel that always goes out with his master when he is walking, that lies down at the couch when Dr. Fuller is taking a ten-minute siesta at noon, and will not even wag his tail while his master sleeps, and who enjoys nothing more than getting into the station wagon and driving off with the family.

This servant of God is not what would be called a hard student. Whatever books he may have read in the past, he is not a great reader of books today. (I am not sure that any great evangelist of our century has been a devourer of books.) He reads the daily papers avidly, and the news weeklies. When he walks out in the evening for the last editions of the day, he will sometimes come home with three different papers. He was a pupil, and a friend and admirer, of Dr. R. A. Torrey, as we have said, but he is not a student as Dr. Torrey was. On the other hand, I would say he is more keenly sensitive to world events, to the deeper meanings of the currents now flowing in our strange world, economic, religious, governmental, than most distinguished preachers of our day. He prepares his messages carefully, but his study is the Word of God. He reads only that he might keep fresh in the messages from which millions draw nourishment week after week.

There is one thing that all will notice who have had any close fellowship with Charles Fuller, and that is his years of international broadcasting, and the great crowds that come to hear him everywhere, have not puffed him up. He almost never speaks of himself, and when he does, it is not in any boastful manner, which seems to attend some of God's servants, to the great detriment of their ministry. Only the other evening a guest in our home was mentioning a certain seminary, famous in a former generation, and I said, "Did you know Dr. —— ?" (Let us call him Dr. James Stevens, as far from his name as possible.) "Oh," said our guest, "you mean the great James." When I asked why such a phrase, the reply was, "That is what everyone called him. He seemed to want to impress everyone with his own importance." Dr. Fuller never tries to impress anyone with his importance. As James Denney said years ago, "A man cannot try to be clever in the pulpit, and at the same time be serious with the gospel." I doubt if any man can enter the pulpit and try to make an impression on people and at the same time press home to their hearts the urgency of a decision for Jesus Christ.

While Dr. Fuller has, of course, met many great men, mayors of large cities, governors of states, army officers, financiers, some of them multimillionaires, etc., he is not one who seems to have any desire to be in frequent communication with the great men of the earth. He lives for Christ, and when he is with these men, he has one desire, and that is to bear witness to the Lord Jesus. Though his mail is heavy, much of it is from the common people and from Christian workers; in fact, may this not be true of most of those who are faithfully proclaiming the gospel, even though they be men of international fame. As one thinks about it, in spite of the fact that he traveled around the world, visited England five times, and was the greatest evangelist of the nineteenth century, one does not come across the names of the world-famous, of world rulers, of world potentates in the life of D. L. Moody. Dr. Fuller's greatest joy is not in brushing shoulders with the men whom other men have honored, and certainly not crowding a schedule with social engagements. His throne is the pulpit, his joy is in the Word of God, his life is centered in Christ; and his hope is not in the passing things of this world. The words of St. Paul seem lived out in this disciple's daily life—"Set not your mind on high things, but condescend to things that are lowly. Be not wise in your own conceits." (Rom. 12:16, R.V.)

There is no pretense in Dr. Fuller's life. What he is, he is. Many who have heard him on the other side of the continent come all the way to Long Beach to see him face to face. They have a word of greeting, hold his hand for a moment, and go back to their homes two or three thousand miles away, with a sense of satisfaction and assurance, more desirous than ever of hearing the words that come from his lips. Dr. Fuller does not pretend to be able to do what he cannot do. He is conscious of his own limitations, whatever they might be. Though he has studied Greek, he would not undertake an original exegesis of a Greek text. He does not think he can write books (though probably he could) so he does not attempt to write books. He keeps himself free from long and exhausting committee meetings, though he has had plenty of them in the days gone by. Many decisions, some of far-reaching importance, must be made, and when he makes them, they are final. He is not blown about by the opinions of others. He does not dissipate his energies, and that is one reason why today he has more vigor than many men twenty years younger.

One time, Mrs. Fuller, writing to Dr. Trumbull, made the remark that her beloved husband was "not eloquent." Though he did not mention names, this led Dr. Trumbull to write a very precious editorial paragraph, which I must insert here: "What we call our hindrance may be, in God's sight, a help. The devoted Christian wife of a true minister writes in a personal letter that her husband's ministry is being greatly blessed: 'He is not eloquent,' she says, 'but God certainly is blessing and using him in spite of that fact.' Perhaps God is saying, 'because of that fact.' There was another man who was 'not eloquent.' God asked him to do a great and difficult thing; bring His people out of bondage and into

God's own promised land. Moses raised a 'serious' objection, reminding the Lord: 'I am not eloquent . . . but I am slow of speech, and of a slow tongue' (Ex. 4:10). Somehow this did not seem to discourage God! Patiently, lovingly he answered: 'Go, and I will be with thy mouth, and teach thee what thou shalt say.' The history of the world has been different ever since, because a man who was not eloquent was willing to let God use him. On the other hand, there is little doubt that, if Moses had been a man of remarkable eloquence, probably God could not have used him. Eloquence is often a snare in Christian service, and it is a question whether God can use eloquent men as effectively as those that are not eloquent. Our weakness is more of an asset in God's sight than our 'strength.' To Moses, to Paul, and to all of us incompetent people the Lord says: 'My grace is sufficient for thee: for my strength is made perfect in weakness.' Shall we not answer this gracious word, with joy and thanksgiving: 'Most gladly therefore will I rather glory in my infirmities, that the power of Christ may rest upon me.'"

Charles Fuller is a strong man who can be trusted. He has been made strong through the trials, the tribulations, the work of a servant of God. Paul wrote to Timothy, "Suffer hardship with the gospel according to the power of God" (II Tim. 1:8). Dr. Fuller has suffered this hardship. He has had business reverses, some of them in the early days leaving him in poverty. He has known bitter criticism, and probably never more than in the last two or three years, sometimes from those who were once his friends, sometimes from total strangers. He has known what it is to have people tell terrible lies about him. I sometimes wonder what particular judgment will await those who create falsehoods concerning the servants of God, scatter them, and then leave, too cowardly to stand up for what they are saying. Paul said of himself, "Most gladly therefore will I rather glory in my weaknesses, that the power of Christ may rest upon me. Wherefore I take pleasure in weaknesses, in injuries, in necessities, in persecutions, in distresses, for Christ's sake: for when I am weak, then am I strong" (II Cor. 12:9, 10). All these things Dr. Fuller has from time to time endured. A weak heart muscle troubled him some years ago, but by care, he has overcome it; necessities, meaning extreme conditions of impoverishment, he knew for years at a time; persecutions he has known from the first day he declared he was going to preach a quarter-century ago, and they have not ceased. I have known him so utterly weak he could hardly move, and yet he keeps on for Christ's sake.

He has frequent battles with forces which most servants of God know nothing about. Someone has said of the story that Martin Luther used to see Satan himself in his study, and throw an ink well at him to drive him out, that the reason we do not see Satan in our secret hours more often is that we are not doing the kind of work which Satan wants to crush. I have heard Dr. Fuller say more than once, after a broadcast, "I felt the very demons themselves contending with me this afternoon as I was preaching the gospel. They seemed to be trying to close my lips and befog my mind. I had a terrible struggle to get through that half-hour."

All this means that, like other men doing great things for God, Dr. Fuller must live much of his life alone. Even when with people, he is living alone. The biographer of A. B. Simpson, founder of the Christian and Missionary Alliance, said that the great crisis in Dr. Simpson's life "led him into the rugged, lonely path which they must tread who fully follow the Lord," and reports that one of his last personal remarks to the students at Nyack was, "I have lived a lonely life."

Never, I think, has Dr. Fuller ever become fanatical on any one subject of the Christian faith. He frequently preaches on prophecy, but he has never set dates, and would shrink from anyone who tried to set them. He believes in holy living, but has never gone off on what we call the tangent of perfection and extreme holiness. He has never sought the gift of tongues. He does not attempt to heal people with the laying on of hands, nor recommend it to anyone else. While he does not criticize those who claim to have these gifts, he has never been discovered dabbling in these side issues of the Christian faith. His message is sane and balanced. If there is any one theme he would emphasize, it is the one which Paul emphasized, "God forbid that I should glory, save in the cross of our Lord Jesus Christ."

One aspect of Dr. Fuller's life is known only to those who have daily contact with him, and that is his extreme thoughtfulness, his kindness to his friends even at a cost of time and energy. I remember not long ago when one of the members of the faculty of the seminary was absent in a city about one hundred miles away, preaching Saturday night and Sunday morning, returning by train to Los Angeles about seven o'clock Sunday night, as no train from that particular city where he was speaking stopped in Pasadena. The only way to get home from Los Angeles, twelve miles away, would be by taxicab. Imagine his astonishment in getting off the train, and walking down the long station platform into the waiting room, to see Dr. Fuller, who had driven to Los Angeles solely to pick up one of his faculty. And remember, Dr. Fuller had that afternoon driven twenty-five miles each way to Long Beach, over one of the most crowded highways in America, and had been on the platform for two hours in his preliminary service and the coast-to-coast broadcast.

I know almost nothing of the inner spiritual life of Dr. Fuller. If I did, I probably would not write about it. He is not one who talks about his own hours alone with God, or who speaks, publicly, of his times of wrestling in prayer. One thing everyone recognizes—every hour he is awake he is seeking to find and do the will of God, and anything that prevents the carrying out of that will must go. The Psalmist said, "In thy light shall I see light" (Ps. 36:9). I think this is the text by which Dr. Fuller judges everything. Whatever he does, whatever he plans, whatever he says, the letters he writes, the conversations he carries on, the friends with whom he has fellowship, his travels, his reading, all must contribute toward one end—the preaching of the gospel for the saving of the souls of men. This makes him intolerant, as the New Testament means intolerance, of clergy and Christian workers who deny the deity and saving work of the Lord Jesus Christ. Paul said, as he closed his first letter to the Corinthians. "If any man loveth not the Lord, let him be anathema." Dr. Fuller would say the same thing. He is a living example of Paul's admonition to the Galatians, "If any man preacheth unto you any gospel other than that which ye received, let him be anathema" (Gal. 1:9). He is not at home with any group that is unfaithful to the high calling of God in Christ Jesus.

When our Lord was on earth, He said, "If any man serve me, let him follow me: and where I am, there shall also my servant be. If any man serve me, him will the Father honor" (John 12:26). This man has served the Lord. He seeks to follow whithersoever the Lord leadeth. Where the Lord is, there does His servant ever want to be. For this reason has the Father honored this man who has lived to honor God's only begotten Son.

www.ingramcontent.com/pod-product-compliance
Lightning Source LLC
Chambersburg PA
CBHW051045160426
43193CB00010B/1070